Introduction

This new LandCraft title charts the essential story of the Jeep during its defining years 1940–45. The Jeep is a 'car' and, something more than that, it has not just touched the lives of millions of people, but it is also a true icon that played a significant role in the course of world history during the Second World War. Over 20 per cent of the vehicles used across the Second World War were Jeeps.

The Jeep and its civilian derivatives also went on to set down the ingredients of the off-road and 4x4 movement that became a design fashion that is still influential upon our motoring. If the Supermarine Spitfire, the Avro Lancaster, and the Boeing B-17 can all be cited as vital to the outcome of the Second World War, then we must surely cite the Jeep in that tribute. Without the Jeep, the great land battles of Europe, North Africa and the Pacific, may well have taken a different turn. In 1991 the Jeep was cited as an International Historic Mechanical Engineering Landmark by the American Society of Mechanical Engineers. More recently a Jeep named 'Sarge' starred in Disney's movie *Cars*. So the Jeep is more than an icon, it is a character and a hero.

The new experimental vehicle of 1940 which became the 'Jeep' via various claims of origination to its name, did not become a named Jeep brand until the 1950s – one that continues to this day. Yet it is the origins of the Bantam Blitz prototype and the Willys Quad, and Ford Pygmy projects that created the combination of design thoughts that ultimately framed the original Jeep concept. This process provided us with the most interesting story and a vehicle which was something more than a car, and one of great influence.

Basic, but a true star of industrial design, the Jeep would become a wartime hero, and went on to inspire a brand. But it was the original 'GP' or 'Jeep' that created military

Willys Jeep in its element.

success for mechanically mounted armies, and it sparked off today's off-road and four-wheel-drive (4x4) enthusiasm across a civilian context. Jeeps were used by the American armed forces, the British, and many other nations: even the Soviet forces

The classic Jeep scene. Note wire cutter beam on front bumper and full equipment.

received several thousand Jeeps under the Lend-Lease Act during the Second World War. Soon afterwards, the French would deploy the Jeep in the Algerian conflict. So

Second World War Airfield Operations/Rescue-equipped Jeep with B-17 in background. (Photo: Deacon AMD 4x4)

Modern Jeep enthusiasm: British-Airborne-forces-marked Jeep fly's the flag.

Jeep truly was a global tool. Operations in the European, North African, Chinese and in the Pacific theatres were the major part of the Jeep story.

From the original Jeep's adaptable, utilitarian, four-wheel-drive design stemmed the idea for off-road, easy-to-use vehicles that ranged from the Land Rover to Japanese 4x4s. 'Agile', small, four-wheel-drive cars have their roots in the Jeep concept.

The key point of the story is that the Jeep was the *first* true, mass-produced four-wheel-drive multi-purpose vehicle – a fact perhaps somewhat obscured from one angle by the reputation of the latterly conceived Land Rover which was not so much a copy, but a British repurposing of the concept.

Correctly framed as an all-American legend, a huge global enthusiasm for the Jeep, its history, restoration, use and modelling, exists. This vehicle has a massive following; the British have great affection for and interest in the Jeep, as do Brazilians, Australians, Indians, and Europeans. The French and the Dutch especially love their Jeeps. Of course, in America, birthplace of the Jeep, the legend and the nation stand together as always.

Originating from an American Austin and a derivative American Bantam idea, the outcome that was the Willys Jeep, the Ford-built Jeep, was latterly to become part of the Kaiser-Willys Corporation, the Kaiser Jeep Corporation, the American Motors Corporation (AMC), then to latterly become part of Chrysler. Production of CJ-series-derived civilian Jeeps in the late 1940s would continue in Argentina, Brazil, India and the Philippines for several decades.

Today, there is huge interest in the original GP-series Jeep and the restoring of Jeeps. A global Jeep enthusiasm exists: Jeeps are huge fun to drive too, even if hot, cold, damp and draughty, and being given to oversteer.

Modellers also study the Jeep in all its variations and details. Tamiya and Airfix are of course, associated with excellent modern-era Jeep models. Yet we should not forget other model manufacturers and the fact that models of the Jeep have been around for many decades – they have become collectables – like the full-size Jeeps. With varying liveries and markings, added kit, armour and armament, a plethora of Jeeps existed and now offer the owner and the modeller wide scope.

The story of the first Jeep and its origins amid a wartime context provides the enthusiast with detailed design interest and an enduring fascination of a true legend. This book, focusing as it does on the essential wartime Jeep and its story of 1940–45, delivers to the enthusiast and the modeller a detailed yet concise narrative to a vital chapter in the history of man's addiction to the motor vehicle and its contribution to history.

Development & Design

The original American Bantam company prototype No 1. Harold Crist and Karl Probst are in the cab, while the design and engineering team is in the background. (Photo QMC/DoD)

Trans-Atlantic Origins

The Jeep has its roots in the genesis of the American automotive industry. The names of Willys, Willys-Knight, Willys-Overland of Toledo, Ohio, as companies and incorporated corporations, can be found in the ancestry of the events that contributed to the reality of the Jeep. Yet the Bantam company, and the Bantam Austin group *must* be cited as the originating part of the Jeep DNA.

Prior to the Bantam contribution, John North Willys had become involved with the 'Overland'-type car in 1907 and by 1914 had formed a Willys-Overland company to design and build a range of cars in the 1920s. Knight sleeve-valve engines would also feature. The Willys company would profit from rapid development and income from making a range of vehicles that were supplied in the latter stages of the First World War of 1914–18. Intriguingly, a light-truck was supplied to the military by Willys, yet Willys would encounter financial issues in 1920 and was soon under the control of a certain Walter P. Chrysler at the behest of Willys backers and the banks behind it. Yet John N. Willys would go on to recover control of his brand in the early 1920s.

Ever the thinker, John N. Willys toured Europe in the late 1920s and returned with a shipment of small 'light' cars then popular on the eastern side of the Atlantic Ocean. Intriguingly, the Willys-Overland company had also made an early foray in the 1920s into the British market by linking up with the Crossley company at Heaton Chapel near Stockport, to assemble a small number of Knight sleeve-valve-engined cars of American origination.

The cars that John Willys brought back from Europe to evaluate were British and French; they created the beginnings of small, nimble cars and the Willys 'Whippet' was the main model John Willys came up with; it may have encouraged the development of the smaller car and its market in the U.S.

The American Austin and the American Austin Bantam companies would benefit from observing such developments and these would lead to the Bantam-produced light car, the 'Blitz' – becoming the Jeep itself – which the Willys company (by then under new ownership) would go on to build and champion and which Ford would have more than a hand in.

Joseph W. Frazer, the great American auto magnate, was also part of the Willys story of the 1920s, and again, after the Jeep had carved its wartime niche, would, like other earlier figures in the 1920s and 1930s, reappear as a figure that was present in the Kaiser-Frazer automotive story. The Willys Jeepster was a post-war direct, original Jeep derivative that sold in the U.S. and in Brazil and it came under the grand marketing bubble of the Kaiser Manufacturing concern which in 1953 bought a major holding in the Willys company. So was born a Kaiser-Willys division of the Willys company. Of note during the Second World War, Kaiser proposed a lightweight, airborne 'Midget' Jeep

It is reputed that this move in 1953 scuppered a plan to licence-build Jeeps in Great Britain by Standard (latterly Standard Triumph Ltd.). But for this we might have seen a Coventry-built Jeep. Land Rover must have been relieved that such a plan did not come to fruition. Similarly, in the 1940s, plans for a British licence-built lightweight version of the 4x4 Jeep with truncated front and rear sections (ideal for airborne/air-drop operations), and lightened body metal gauge, with lowered engine height, were drawn up by the Nuffield concern that owned the Morris marque but curiously came to nothing.

How ironic it would have been to have seen a British-built 'Morris' Jeep given that the Jeep's origins lie, via the Austin Seven being licence-built in America (and Japan and Germany) and forming the basis of the American Bantam, and via the studies and cars of John North Willys, *all* of which led to the Jeep in the first place. And the proposed British assembly of Willys-Overland Crossley cars of the late 1920s, would have been the precursors.

During the Second World War, Willys, and Ford of Detroit, would become synonymous with the Jeep and its development. Yet the *original* engineering and design roots of the first 'GP' type car that became the Jeep itself, stem from Austin of England and a deal to licence-build Austin Sevens as American cars in America via the American Austin, and the American Bantam companies. So, via Austin, the Jeep truly has a touch of international blood. The reader might care to search out images of the 1930s Austin Seven Light Special – an open-topped, short wheelbase roadster – notably in the body tub, scuttle, cutaway sides and rear panels, details which really do remind us of the Jeep's (more upright) body design that came along just a few years later.

Paradoxically, the very first, earliest 1947 Land Rover prototype looks *more* like a Jeep than the 1949 production Land Rover design. The initial prototype Land Rover body (built of alloy) had curved front wings (or fenders), and curved pressings for the rear wings and cutaway, doorless sides. It even had a fold-down windscreen mounted on a tubular frame attached to the front wings – almost identical to the Jeep's design. Land Rover would soon invoke a more individual windscreen frame design and a new front grill and headlamp design treatment too. And the Belgian Minerva-produced steel-bodied Land Rover Series One also has a more visual 'Jeepness'.

Little known in the wider 4x4 story was the influence of the late 1940s cooperation between Northern Ireland's Harry Ferguson and the Ford Motor Company in the development of tractor design and four-wheel-drive engineering. Even less obvious in post-war Great Britain was another man from Northern Ireland – Rex McCandless,

Detail of the original design – note the curved front panel, slat/bar grill and wing/fender design. (Photo QMC/DoD)

a maverick engineer who was interested in 500cc racers, 'Specials', and who, in 1949 designed a small, military-use four-wheel-drive, backbone-chassised vehicle known as the 'Mule'. Harry Ferguson was involved in the prototype development of this – a car which could have been a direct, British-designed competitor to the Jeep. But only one was built and by 1952 the project was dead. So Jeep got there first and had the world at its feet – with Land Rover following closely in its wheel tracks.

The *original* idea for a go-anywhere, adaptable, simple lightweight, agile car (which created the Jeep) had its roots in an American iteration of a 1930s British Austin design that inspired a 'Bantam'-type car with good ground clearance, simple construction and ease of use. Other influences came from the developments in the American automotive industry circa 1925–39: of note, the Jeep's L-head 2.2-litre engine had its roots in a 1927-dated engine design used in the Willys-Overland company's 'Whippet' car.

Parallel developments in the 1930s saw hill-climb cars and hot rods and one-off or limited production 'Specials' being built in the U.S. and in Great Britain. Of note: the British Army used a modified Austin saloon chassis as a minimally bodied light-duties utility vehicle.

All of these small cars in the 1930s were short-wheelbase, low-build, high-ground-clearance devices (with capable suspension for use as off-road hill-climbers), two-seat open cabins, and minimal bodywork tubs bolted to a strong central chassis frame. Clearly, such themes, however civilian orientated, *would* contribute to the mindset and the development of a multi-purpose vehicle of military use in the late 1930s and to the Jeep itself.

Of significance in the U.S. military journey to procure the Jeep, there was a trail of vehicles that we might call precursors to the outcome.

As early as 1903, the Dutch Spyker concern had built an all-wheel or four-wheel-drive car, but it was steam-powered. An early American deployment of the all-wheel-drive system came from the 'FWD Wagon Company' that also experimented with four-wheel steering.

In the First World War, the U.S. Army had used four-wheel-drive trucks, and several manufacturers had built four-wheel-drive tractors. In 1936 the Marmon-Herrington company modified several Fords to four-wheel-drive 1½-ton design and submitted them for U.S. Army evaluation: the device was deemed to be too heavy. Of note: a four-wheel-drive Miller took part in the 1932 motor race at no less a venue than Indianapolis. Farmers meanwhile, were soon experimenting with tractors that deployed drive to all the wheels.

Between 1925 and 1937, modified Model T and Model A Fords with cutaway bodies were popular with farmers and with builders of 'Specials' in the 1930s. It would be a couple of short steps to re-imagine or re-purpose such vehicles for another role. Indeed, in 1924, the U.S. Ordnance Department examined a Ford Model T that had been given off-road 'balloon' tyres, a front axle diff/drive mechanism and a canvas folding roof or tilt. Was this the still-born ancestor of the thinking that created the Jeep over a decade later?

In 1935, in a publication known as the *American Cavalry Journal*, a design for a 'lightweight cross-country car' was proposed (with drawings) by a Lt H. G. Hamilton. Is he a forgotten contributor to the Jeep legend?

Another ancestor of all such designs and of the Jeep may be cited as the little-known Howie-Wiley 'Belly Flopper' when, in 1937, two army men, Major R. G. Howie, and Master Sergeant M. C. Wiley, built a single 'Special' as an off-roader with an Austin Seven engine (from Bantam). They followed European design trends of that era by mounting the engine in the rear (but driving the front wheels). The body was less than four feet high and the two-man crew were to lie prone, one driving, one firing the armament. This light car used an American Bantam-type chassis based on the Austin Seven to which was added an above-the-chassis baseplate tub or platform.

Several public demonstrations of the so-called Belly Flopper were given within the American motor industry and to the motoring press. But was the under-wheeled Howie-Wiley Belly Flopper the first real attempt at a light utility for the American military in the mid-1930s? The prototype failed for a lack of traction: all the weight was over the non-driving wheels. So thoughts soon turned to all-wheel drive and a nimble, military 'car'. Major Howie would soon join the Ordnance Department's Technical Committee and therefore assess and influence the subsequent Bantam-Willys Jeep process itself, in 1940.

Many of military bent were, it seems, thinking about a small military all-rounder of a light car.

All-wheel-drive trucks and tractors had existed in America and a Marmon-Herrington 4x4 light truck based on a Ford Model LD1 was proposed in 1937. This was the first such concept vehicle to be assessed at Camp Holabird and, by 1939, a small order for 64 examples was placed with W. C. Marmon's company. The design went no further but some call it an ancestor to the Jeep itself.

Citroën of France had experimented with off-road vehicles, notably the Kegresse half-tracked series. Bugatti had also considered a four-wheel-drive system for its later racing types. In Great Britain, the famous 1930s trials and hill-climb driver Sydney Allard had built half a dozen off-road 'Specials' between 1936 and 1939 using American-originated Ford engines and components with great success and, as

Early Willys development chassis. Note the grill, body side apeture shape and the difference in the production design of the front wing/fender. (Photo: US National Archive)

early as 1938, Allard had created a high-ground-clearance, four-wheel-drive, light car-cum utility design that he suggested was ideal for military transport and general duties use. But the government of the day turned him and his big idea down, after he had actually supplied the Ministry of Supply with full, costed, engineered plans and details using existing Ford parts.

Sydney Allard's forgotten 1937 design for a Ford-derived light, utility, agile 4x4 for the military suddenly seems not only prescient, but also another example of how brilliant British ideas got lost in the torpor of the British mindset of the 1930s – not unlike the development of the Whittle jet engine. In fact, in 1932, the British Army had modified an Austin saloon into a higher-ground-clearance car for army use, but it lacked four-wheel drive. A one-off private four-wheel-drive agile or scout-type car was suggested in 1935 by a British officer, but it was Allard who drew up, specified and planned a proper, high-ground-clearance, all-terrain, four-wheel-drive agile car for military use.

So it was left to the Americans to create and to perfect the great device that became the Jeep.

Some historians may argue that the Russians produced the GAZ (Gorkovsky Avtomobilny Zavod) 4x4 first, but this was a converted saloon car. Only after 1941 did GAZ's version of the Jeep concept become reality. This was the R1 and then came the GAZ 61–64 series of light 4x4 scout-car/transport vehicles, essentially Jeep 'copies' made heavier and more rugged to deal with local conditions. Not for the last time a Russian vehicle would be a copy of a western design.

And Russian competition came from the N.A.T.I. Research Institute, who had designed their own prototype with many similarities to the GAZ. Moskivich also made four-wheel-drive cars before 1941, but these were military *conversions* based upon pre-existing road-car components.

All-wheel drive they may have been, but they were not yet dedicated designs as purpose-built vehicles. GAZ would produce the defining Russian 4x4 as the GAZ 60-series.

In Britain, within two years of Sydney Allard's idea for a Ford-based agile 4x4 being turned down, the Jeep had filled the void so stupidly ignored by the British government. The Land Rover would come belatedly as a reverse-engineered piece of genius to British minds, as would a then contemporary luxury-trimmed version of the early Land Rover built by Tickford Ltd. – 250 were built – something truly prescient for the 4x4 market of three decades later. And how coincidental that it should be the giant Ford Motor Company that would indeed be part of a 4x4 story via the Jeep – not the Allard Ford-based idea of just three years earlier.

Post-war, Austin would also create its own version of a 'Jeep' – in an ironically belated piece of Austin–Bantam reverse engineering. Yet it was the American Bantam company of the 1930s that successfully suggested a modified, cut-down roadster could form the suitable basis of a military-use light car: an agile car. Although no single person invented the 'Jeep' light carrier concept (which had been toyed with since the early 1920s), we must cite Bantam as the *true* originators of the actual design that defined that concept as a production item.

Bantam Origins

Prior to the American Bantam Company, there was in its corporate development the earlier American Austin Company Inc., of Butler, Pennsylvania. This original company had from 1930 licence-built the British Austin Seven re-clothed in a contemporary American-fashioned body of simple and utilitarian style and ability. The car sold for just $10 dollars more than the ubiquitous 'go-anywhere' Model A Ford. By 1932 the British Austin-derived project had closed and yet the vehicle's rights were soon owned and reincarnated by a car dealer, one Roy Evans of Georgia, who produced another 5,782 examples up to June 1934.

The Austin-originated little car was then reborn for a *second* time in late 1937 under the name of the American Bantam Company, Inc. New styling took the original Austin-derived Bantam away from its simple, economy-car roots and created a small, but very stylish little car that even boasted rear-wheel spats and a convertible roadster version.

Intriguingly, we can see more of the Jeep's body style and high-ground-clearance, short-wheelbase style in the original 'upright' 1930-designed American Austin-type sedan than we can in its late re-modelled Bantam saloon and roadster which was more 'designer' in its attempt at a swept, 'streamliner', late-1930s-era style. The humble Austin Bantam origins were completely disguised by the car's Alex de Sakhnoffsky styling.

A revised engine design by Harry. A. Miller took the car further away from its light car DNA of Austin. By 1940, 4,025 Bantams would be built. But although this car died in late 1940, it must be cited as a strain in the direct DNA of the next car that the American Bantam Company, Inc. developed: the general-purpose iteration that soon became the true wartime Jeep.

Harry Miller had long thought about a four-wheel-drive vehicle, as had Harry Ferguson, and both would touch the Jeep story. Miller would become Bantam's vice-president and bring his personal motor racing experience to the Jeep project. One of his engineers at Jeep would be a time-served race engineer formerly of the revered Stutz company, one Harold Crist. So Bantam had racing engineering on hand to develop its agile, fast scout car.

A civilian engineer working for the Quartermaster Dept was a Mr Robert Brown and he would work with Bantam and Harold Crist on the early designs of the prototype of what became the Jeep. Mr Chester Hempfling and a Mr Ralph Turner are cited as the two lead mechanics who worked on the prototype.

The Austin–Bantam process, overseen by F. H. Fenn as company president, was how the evolved American Austin–Bantam Company came to create the light car/ reconnaissance vehicle that became the so-called 'Blitz Buggy' as a precursor to the GP and then the basis of the 'combined' Jeep design. Mr A. Brandt had previously run Bantam and in collaboration with Fenn, he recruited the designer Karl Probst to devise the new light, agile vehicle.

This period was the famous 'five days' in 1940 when Probst drew up and delivered, on 22 July, the Bantam plans for the vehicle and agreed the use of existing parts-bin components such as the Spicer rear axle (as also used by Studebaker) and as many sundry parts as possible. After submission, Probst would have the final tooling drawings ready for 21 September. But the prototype's weight had crept over 800lb – well over the army's specified target. Yet this was to be the lightest of the three competing prototypes and most of the weight came from the Continental-sourced, iron-block engine.

August saw Bantam awarded the contract and given until 21 September to deliver the first single, rolling prototype to the army's testing facility at Camp Holabird where two months of evaluation would ensue. Willys and Ford were on site and allowed to see the secret Bantam prototype in what would ordinarily have been a massive breach of commercial confidentiality and security in peacetime, but which the army had no problem with; Bantam were aggrieved but there was little they could do.

Bantam were not alone in their attempts to create a useful all-terrain, lightweight car-cum-truck. Yet the cut-down Bantam roadster with added lightness was the real genesis of the Bantam light military car design that became the Jeep.

Drawn up in 1940 to a U.S. Military Quartermaster Corps requirement for a 4x4 light truck of 'quarter-ton' context, thus came the urgently needed light transport and go-anywhere vehicle that could also be deployed as a fast, cross-country reconnaissance type. It was conceived and prototyped in a matter of weeks after the U.S. Army Technical Committee formalized its specification requirements in July 1940, and offered them to the U.S. automotive manufacturers.

Committee members included Major Howie, and Messrs W. Beasley, R. Brown, and W. Burgan. These men defined the parameters of weight, speed, armament, power, and capacity for the proposed Jeep and are even reputed to have drawn up a rough sketch of what they were looking for.

The U.S. Army's need was urgent, even if America had not yet entered the war. Europe was erupting as the Nazi war machine invaded all but Great Britain. Pearl Harbor may have been just over a year away, but the need for military equipment to support a U.S. entry into the war was obvious.

Design tenders were to be received by 22 July 1940. Manufacturers were given just 49 days to submit their prototypes and 75 days for completion of their test vehicles. The Quartermaster's office oversaw the Ordnance Technical Committee specifications which were clear: the vehicle would be four-wheel drive, have a complement of three-crew on a wheelbase of no more than 75 inches (191cm) which was soon increased to 80 inches (203cm). The track had to be less than 47 inches (119cm), and the body weight less than 1,300lb (590kg), although this proved to be too self-limiting and was amended in curious circumstances that the army was unqualified to control. 2,156lb or 980kg would soon become the working figure.

Willys test chassis 1. Note the WILLYS branded front valance and the curved wing/ fender supports. The design includes three wooden blocks on the bonnet for folding windscreen support – changed to two for the production version. From here it was just one more step to a defining design. (Photo: Dept of Defense)

Highly articulate suspension with good ground clearance, a tight turning circle, and short front and rear overhangs to permit easy entry and exit angle clearances on rough terrain were key factors. So too was mud-plugging torque.

Critical off-road factors for the design were framed thus:

Approach angle: 45°
Exit Angle: 35°
Water fording depth: 45cm (18in)
Payload: 360kg (795lb)
Total weight (4WD): 999kg (2,200lb)
Minimum 'crawler' speed: 4kph (2.5mph)
Maximum 'dash' speed: 90kph (55mph)
Four-wheel drive

The U.S. military's civilian engineers from Bantam, and Ford and Willys are often said to have collaborated in the Jeep's design, but the Jeep may be less of a design-by-committee than some authors now claim. After all, Bantam had suggested a military light-car product and had designed and built the early prototype of what became the first 'Blitz' car in 1940, and the re-imagined roadster utility prototype had been key. Willys by contrast had asked for extra time, a total of 75 days, whereas Bantam had delivered their plans on time and built a prototype ready for testing by September 1940 at the U.S. Army test centre in Maryland.

So Bantam's light car/truck was designed in less than a week by Karl Probst and soon tagged the 'BRC' or Bantam Reconnaissance Car, but it had a failing – a low-powered and heavy engine that was lacking in the torque vital for any all-terrain and fast-road vehicle.

Willys would develop their prototype as the 'Quad' (thence as 'Standard Truck 4x4') which was overweight too, but Willys would soon have the opportunity to solve the Bantam engine's power-to-weight-ratio

The famous PR shot – the prototype lobbies Washington D.C. By traversing the steps of the State building. (Photo DoD)

issue as part of the army's manufacturing contract, with the fitting of a larger 2.2-litre 55hp/ 60hp-capacity engine – the 441, or, 442 'Go-Devil'. With over 105lb/ft (142Nm) of torque this was the ideal engine; it boasted over 30lb/ft torque more than the Ford engine or the Bantam's Continental-sourced engine. Delmar G. Roos would be the engineering mind that was behind the Willys Go-Devil engine that transformed the early under-powered Bantam Jeep.

Bantam must have been concerned when the U.S. government passed on its designs for the car to Willys (and Ford), the government claiming ownership and national interest as justifying such a move that would normally have seen the originating manufacturer issuing proceedings.

Indeed, of direct relevance, there would occur a legal argument about who created the Jeep. In 1948, the U.S. Federal Trade Commission sided with American Bantam Company and its claim that the idea of creating the Jeep's design context had indeed been *originated* and developed by the American Bantam Company Inc. But the Trade Commission added that this had occurred in collaboration with the U.S. Army Corps, and cited the four-wheel-drive transfer case engineers, the Spicer Company, as part of that development. Strangely, while citing a Ford contribution, the Trade Commission denied the Willys Company from claiming (directly or by implication) that *it* had thought up the Jeep. However Willys' development of the Jeep (and its re-engine of it) was cited.

By the time this legal decision of 1948 had set its precedent, the Bantam Company would soon go bankrupt, in late 1949 – just as the post-war civilian Jeep market boom started: Willys ended up with a pyrrhic victory and ownership of the Jeep name.

Prior to this, back in 1940, there was an intervention by the OPM, the Office of Production Management. This was because it became clear that powerful forces were at work to grab the contract and the basic design away from its originator (Bantam) and hand it to big business. Indeed Bantam's senior director, Mr Payne, took his case to Secretary of State for War Henry Stimson. Lobbying, vested interests and power were all at play for this lucrative prize contract. The General Staff subsequently awarded Bantam the initial deal and then awarded Willys their development and manufacture contract. Ford, of course, soon won the day, after each – Willys and Bantam – had built an initial batch of 1,000-plus so-called Jeeps.

Willys Quad: Ford Pygmy

Back in the closing months of 1940, Edsel Ford, Henry Ford's son and man of ideas and eager dynamism, had decided that Ford would produce its own version of the called-for official army specification – the Ford 'Pygmy'. Edsel's nationally powerful father Henry Ford lobbied important people for Ford to be involved – reputedly citing Bantam's production limitations and small-scale funding. Edsel Ford would be dead by 1943: the Ford family's effect in the portals of power circa 1941–42 cannot go uncited in the circumstances that saw the Bantam-designed 'Jeep' become a Ford-manufactured item via a Willys iteration. Put simply, beyond patriotism, Ford wanted the business and had friends in high places. Of note: Ford had discussed and drawn up a contract for a joint concern in the USSR for the building of a joint Ford–GAZ factory for light truck production in Russia in 1929. There should be little surprise in the discovery that some subsequent GAZ components in the 1930s were re-purposed Ford toolings.

Ford's early-build version of the Jeep-type specification, had distinctively curved, one-piece front wing mudguard/fender panels and a deep, curved side access cutaway aperture on both sides of the tub to allow ingress and egress from the two front seats. These were significant differences in appearance and metalwork that identified the early-build Ford Pygmy and the early production version.

Willys, under chief designer D. G. Ross, would produce a version of their specification that was initially solely rear-wheel drive (but which was soon modified into an all-wheel-drive 4x4 status), being tagged, the Quad. Willys would produce the 'lead' type but in the final outcome, the Ford-type frontal design would be incorporated into the Willys version of what became the jointly produced Jeep.

Willys would also build 10 Jeep prototypes with rear-wheel steering – an often forgotten event.

Both initial prototypes would be absorbed into the combined specification that became the Willys Military Type (A) – generally seen as the origin of the lighter model and the MA-MB series Jeep yet which would merge into the consequent Ford-built production series under the auspices of the generic 'Jeep' type – *whoever* manufactured it (with many components being interchangeable). MA defined the Military Model A. The MB was the wider production version.

Prior to Willys–Ford production, the Ford 1940 prototype, the Quad, used a version of the Ford side-valve 2-litre tractor engine (itself part of a Ford–Ferguson engineering and manufacturing agreement signed by Ford and Harry Ferguson, the Northern Irish tractor manufacturer. Ford and Ferguson would eventually become embroiled in a long-running legal case over certain design rights); the Quad became the GP – from Government contract Type, of P status – which was an internal Ford code. The Ford Model A gearbox was used by Ford, which, like Bantam, had also selected the Spicer axles.

The original Bantam prototype evolved into a revised version. But Bantam as we

know, were said to have lacked the factory capacity to churn out its car. The U.S. Army is said to have voiced 'concerns' that Bantam could not fill the contract because it was too small to do so. But an independent audit reputedly showed that Bantam and the affiliated Butler plants *could* have produced over 200,000 units per annum. But Bantam were cash-limited and needed to win the contract in order to fund the ordering of the parts (notably the Spicer components), to build the Jeeps to meet the contract. It was a Catch-22 situation, and many feel that Ford made the most of the issues by being in a position to offer unlimited funding and resources on a grand scale and lobbying the government to prod the army to pass the project to Ford.

Was skulduggery at work? Did Ford lobby behind the scenes to get the U.S. Army to pressure the U.S. government to use its power to take the Jeep project away from Bantam by citing Bantam's limitations? Given that Bantam (and then Willys) effectively lost control of the project by official order, and that Ford effectively took over large-scale wartime production,

The classic elements of the production Jeep as seen by the QMC's publications.

WAR DEPARTMENT LUBRICATION GUIDE No. 501
ORDNANCE DEPARTMENT

TRUCK, ¼ TON, 4x4 (FORD-WILLYS)

SNL G-503. For detailed instructions, refer to TM.

TABLE OF CAPACITIES AND LUBRICANTS TO BE USED

UNIT	CAPACITY (Approx.)	LOWEST EXPECTED AIR TEMPERATURE		
		+32°F. and above	+32°F. to 0°F.	Below 0°F.
Crankcase (Including Oil Filter)	5 qt.	OE SAE 30	OE SAE 10	Refer to OFSB 6-11
Transmission	¾ qt.	GO SAE 90	GO SAE 80	GO Grade 75
Transfer Case	1½ qt.			
Differentials (each)	1¼ qt.			

CAUTION — Lubricate Dotted Arrow Points on BOTH SIDES. Points on OPPOSITE SIDE are indicated by Dotted Short-Shaft Arrows.

NOTE — See Reverse Side for lubrication of TRAILER.

Serviced From Engine Compartment

Lubricant • Interval

- Spring Shackle CG 1
- Front Axle Differential GO 6 — Drain and refill Check level weekly. (Note 7)
- Shock Absorbers SA 6 — (Some models) (Notes 15 and 16)
- Tie Rod CG 1
- Tie Rods (Inner) CG 1
- Front Wheel Bearings WB 6 — Remove, clean and repack
- Universal Joint and Steering CG 1 — Knuckle Bearings (Note 8)
- Drag Link CG 1
- Steering Bellcrank CG 1
- Universal Joint CG 1 — (Note 9)
- Spring Bolt CG 1
- Drag Link CG 1
- Clutch and Brake Pedals CG 1
- Transmission GO 6 — Drain and refill (Early WILLYS Models right side) Check level weekly. (Notes 15 and 16)
- Spring Bolt CG 1
- Rear Wheel Bearings WB 6 — Remove, clean and repack
- Shock Absorbers SA 6 — (Some models) (Notes 15 and 16)
- Rear Axle Differential GO 6 — Drain and refill Check level weekly. (Note 7)
- Spring Shackle CG 1

Interval • Lubricant

- 1 Oil Filter (Note 5)
- 1 OE Generator (Early models) (Note 15)
- 1 OE Crankcase (See Table) — Drain and refill Check level weekly
- 1 OE Distributor Shaft
- 6 OE Distributor (Note 10)
- 1 OE Starter
- D OE Air Cleaner (Note 4) — 6 to 8 drops Check level weekly
- 1 GO Steering Gear
- 1 HB Brake Master Cylinder (Remove cover on toeboard) — Fill to ½ in. from top
- 1 CG Universal and Slip Joints (Note 9)
- 1 CG Trans. Case Shift Lever Shaft
- 6 GO Transfer Case — Drain and refill Check level weekly (Note 7)
- 1 CG Universal and Slip Joints (Note 9)

KEY

Lubricants	Intervals
OE—OIL, engine. Except crankcase SAE 30 (above +32°F.) SAE 10 (+32°F. to 0°F.) PS (below 0°F.)	D—Daily
GO—LUBRICANT, gear. See Table	1—1,000 miles
CG—GREASE, general purpose	6—6,000 miles
WB—GREASE, general purpose, No. 2	Check Daily
HB—FLUID, brake, hydraulic	Crankcase
SA—FLUID, shock absorber, light	Air Cleaner
PS—OIL, lubricating, preservative, special	

This official lubrication data sheet and chassis view is noteworthy for its 'Ford-Willys' branding.

we can only presume that whatever the mechanism, the outcome was exactly what Ford would have wanted.

Bantam did turn out two updated prototypes of the original 'Blitz' prototype that had first turned its wheels on 11 July 1940. Today one Bantam Blitz resides in the Smithsonian museum, yet debate over the subsequent two prototypes continues. One may be hiding somewhere in the U.S., or perhaps, as is rumoured, in Canada.

From the three separate but similar prototypes, evaluated by the U.S. Army, came separate development series orders from the army to each manufacturer. Bantam noted just how much the Willys and the Ford iterations resembled their original. Perhaps it was a step taken to mollify Bantam, but they were given the contract to build the 10,000 Jeep-specific trailers that would undertake such sterling service across all theatres of the Second World War: just over 73,000 trailers would be built.

From this came the process that led to the amalgamation to a single, almost-standardized design. Willys, whose manufacturing quote was cheap at under $950, would simply be awarded the production project – adding the larger Willys-originated 2.2-litre engine in the process and various Willys and, then, Ford improvements. Unusually, the car had a steering column-mounted gear change – at a time when side or centre-mounted floor gearbox linkages were coming into fashion. Sadly, the originating Bantam-type basis of the Jeep was phased-out relatively early on in the wartime Jeep story. Ford would soon get the unit cost down to $925 per vehicle.

After building 2,675 early Bantam versions, war production passed to the larger Willys and Ford outfits respectively. These two automotive manufacturing concerns had the capacity to churn out Jeeps by the hundreds of thousands, far beyond the American Bantam Company's abilities and with Ford being of greater capacity than even Willys could manage.

The many Jeep variations that now provide the restorer with head-scratching, and the modeller with challenges stem from these various circumstances and production differences. Curiously, despite all the changes and developments, the final post-1941 Jeep remained remarkably faithful to Karl Probst's original Bantam design with only Probst's curved frontal treatment being the major change, along with the curved side-cutaway tub apertures being reshaped.

So was born the convoluted, and still debated, DNA of the Jeep.

The Willys-built Jeep set the mould, it cast the tooling for a small, nimble off-road, on-road, multi-purpose 4x4 type. The Ford-built Jeep would dominate the production series.

Over 2,000 early Bantam BRCs were offered under Lend-Lease to the British and the Soviet governments respectively, so too were early-build Willys MA and over 3,500 Ford-built variants. These early-production vehicles formed the basis of the Jeeps to be found in Europe as early as 1942. Interestingly, it was the lower-powered but lighter-weight Bantam BRCs that did well in the Western Desert with British forces.

The first series-production Jeeps were recorded as follows:

Bantam BRC Mk II manufactured September 1940–December 1940 with reg nos 2015324–2015393

Willys MA manufactured June 1941–August 1941 with reg nos 2018932–2020431

Ford GP manufactured February 1941–May 1941 with reg nos 2017422–2028921

We might as a point of interest note that by 1942 the Nazis had started building their own experimental four-wheel-drive agile utility car – the 4x4 Volkswagen (VW) 'Beetle' types – with just 564 *Test-wagen* prototypes being constructed. There was also the Dr Porsche-designed all-wheel-drive Schwimm-wagen. There was also the 'German Jeep', the VW Kubelwagen, but it was nothing of the sort of course, because it lacked four-wheel drive, and was a larger, four-door device of VW/Porsche rear-engined, rear-driven technicality. The Kubelwagen's saving grace was that it was air-cooled and therefore easy to

The bones of the Jeep's simple steel pressings are visible here. Note the difference in the under-seat fuel tank location from the standard.

Chassis details reveal the key difference between Willys and Ford front cross members – tubular, or square, according to type.

use and maintain in inhospitable wartime environments: its lethal swing-axle, rear-biased handling was however a 'killer' factor. Unusually amid the great output of Nazi-funded advanced science and technology, the Kubelwagen was less than intelligent.

So came the true 4x4 Jeep to the fore – worldwide and utterly dominant.

What's in a Name?

Was the term 'GP' (to become spoken as geep) derived from 'general purpose' as some say, or from Ford's in-house Government type, P-coded nomenclature? The controversy has ranged for decades and each enthusiast has a specific rationale for believing what they do.

The uncomfortable truth may be that in 1932 the U.S. military discussed its need for a light truck-cum-utility vehicle with numerous external suppliers and potential parties. And yet again a British theme is layered in the history as the British Army had used a modified Austin saloon chassis type for general purpose/messenger/assault duties. Given the American Austin developments at the same time, it is hardly a surprise to note that an example of this modified Austin was evaluated by the U.S. military.

Some people claim that the generic term 'jeep' was in use by American servicemen at this time in the early 1930s. This term 'jeep' was also the name of a popular cartoon character of the 1930s called 'Eugene the Jeep' as found in the *Popeye* cartoons. This 'jeep' was a go-anywhere, do anything mythological animal which could metamorphose itself through structures and any terrain or barrier. Apparently, U.S. servicemen *had* used the theme of such a device or capability as applied to various inanimate mechanical objects including trucks, cars, troop carriers, ships, tools and even aircraft. But they had also called such vehicles 'Peeps', which only added to the confusion.

So there could be a sociological cause to the etymology of the actual, mechanical term 'jeep' long before it was so appropriately applied to the one and only

Front suspension details reveal vital engineering and low centre of gravity.

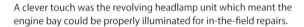

A clever touch was the revolving headlamp unit which meant the engine bay could be properly illuminated for in-the-field repairs.

This original Willys engine bay depicts all the correct fittings and air intake trumpet.

The Willys engine was compact of dimension and high on torque. This close-up depicts how the engine and ancillaries should look when restored to original specification.

true Jeep – which would metamorphose into the Jeep brand of the 1950s. As for Peeps – that too was a real term.

Indeed, what of the farm tractors of the American 1930s, converted to four-wheel drive on an *ad hoc* private basis that led to the idea of a 'prime-mover', a four-wheel-drive artillery towing vehicle created by the Minneapolis Moline Power Implement Company? Many sources cite such vehicles as being termed 'jeeps'. Such a story is far more attractive than the obvious GP or general purpose, that some ascribe as the origins of the *Geep* as Jeep. However, as early as 1941, there are records of the general purpose terminology being applied to the design, so the spoken 'Geep' could have influenced Jeep as a term. No less

a figure than Willys President Joe Frazer claimed to have slurred the word into Geep.

However, the GP (Ford-built)/MA/MB (Willys-built) that became the Jeep was, it is believed, apparently first descriptively applied by the *Washington Daily News* in March 1941, reported after a Willys PR event to drive its new car up the steps of the Capitol building in Washington D.C. It is reputed that the Willys test driver referred to the new vehicle as a Jeep during this demonstration for the national media, hence a cited publication from the *Washington Daily News*.

Records indicate that in February 1942, a Lieutenant-Colonel E. S. Van Deusen, the motor transport (MT) Chief of procurement and Engineering, spoke to the Society of Automobile Engineers in New York and termed the new vehicle as the 'Jeep'.

By July 1941, the U.S. Department of War had ordered 16,000 of the new specification car. Willys had the production capacity and were quite happy to absorb, or reverse-engineer the Bantam design basis, and some Ford ideas, into a Willys-manufactured, Willys-engined car. This became the MA/MB. By November 1941, just before Pearl Harbor (and subsequent increase in demand for the car) it became obvious that even Willys could not meet the numbers required in the time available.

Plans and toolings were simply and quickly shipped by government edict to the Ford works in Detroit and, retaining its own prototype's 'GP' identifier, Ford just added a 'W' for Willys derivation. Hence the Ford

GPW was born and was soon roaring out of the Ford Detroit factory – but crucially, *not* with a Ford engine, but retaining the Willys engine. Ford did not have an engine that was as powerful, torque infused, or as light as the Willys engine. And they could hardly upset the car's entire dynamics and structure by loading the cast-iron lump that was the often hot-running, built-down-to-a-price, under-cooled, Ford flat-head V8 into the little Jeep.

But Ford did not need to worry, for it had secured the vital $14.5-million contract to build the Jeep in 15,000 units: Ford would go on to build 277,896 GPW Jeeps. Early Ford Jeeps used Willys chassis frames, but debate ensues as to up to which GPW number.

Key suppliers to the Jeep project were Auburn Central, Midland Steel, Kelsey-Hayes, and Spicer, which provided the four-wheel-drive transfer mechanicals. As the design was for a U.S. government specification, that government then claimed ownership rights to the Jeep design and awarded itself the patent and rights in April 1942.

In March 1941, the Auburn Central company was awarded a contract to produce 1,600 Jeep bodies for Willys-Overland. From March 1942, Auburn became the American Central Manufacturing Company and was to become the lead manufacturer of Jeep bodies. After the 1941 changes to the Jeep's tub design, further design rationalization of the tub would take place in early 1944.

The Jeep in Detail

Below: Basic instruments were all that was needed.

Bottom: Willys cabin. Note the rifle rack, original lighting switch and location of the gear lever and transfer levers.

So evolved the design language and engineering integrity of the Jeep. The core of the new light car-cum-truck was a basic, twin-rail box-section, cross-braced chassis that was strong yet could absorb suspension loads and torsional twist. The chassis was clad in thin, lightweight steel bodywork that offered a fold-flat windscreen that was also quickly detachable. A single layer of paint became the military specification; after all long-life and rust-proofing were hardly wartime design requirements. Under that paint layer, several variations of primer were used. This included 'Red' ferrous-oxide-based primer. It is now known that some MB Jeeps dated January and February 1942 have been found with original, zinc-chromate primer on the tub and front wings – so production differences and supplier variations were real despite the standardized design.

The ladder-type chassis was manufactured by the Midland Steel Company, under the simple, steel (not aluminium) body panels would soon be found more power in that derivative of a Willys-designed 2.2-litre (2,199cc), 55bhp (then 60bhp) four-cylinder side-valve engine (with aluminium pistons) which replaced the original Continental-sourced engine of approximately 35bhp that was to be found in the first 2,675 American Bantam Company-built 'pilot'-specification cars prior to 1941.

The dashboard or fascia saw traditional vital gauges for fuel contents, volts/ammeter charge, water temperature and of course the largely irrelevant speedometer. The two transfer case/gear levers were

The very useful rear 'bustle' cage could carry fuel cans, spares, kit, bicycles, or booze!

Detail of floor pan and gear levers. Note the left-hand location of the fire extinguisher.

This kind of chassis information was often quickly stencilled onto Jeeps as they were shipped from New York in the war years: it rarely lasted long due to wear and weathering.

FROM U.S. PORT AGENCY
WAR SHIPPING ADM. N.Y.

ROAD WT   2315 LBS.
GROSS WT   3125 LBS.
LENGTH   132 IN.
WIDTH   62 IN.
HEIGHT   52 IN.

a free-wheeling front axle offered great adaptability. Although probably delivering just less than 65bhp in service, the Willys side-valve engine did offer superb torque of 105lb/ft (142Nm) and delivered it at a very usable 2,000 rpm, offering real mud-plugging (and towing) traction abilities ideal for combat terrain the world over. A torque figure of nearly double the horsepower figure indicated a tight, square, strong engine that had great internal efficiency and an excellent drivetrain or transmission to deliver it.

Interestingly, the Ford-built version of the Willys engine used head-to-block studs instead of bolts. Ford favoured studs and had been building up experience on use of studs in their 21-stud flat-head V8 – eventually using 24 studs.

The three-speed transmission was originally of Borg and Beck type 11123 dry-clutch. Synchromesh was on the first and second gears only. A separate lever engaged/disengaged the front-transmission into the drive-line. Low-range gear ratios were also vital – and another lever.

The suspension was simple and like the rest of the vehicle easy to maintain and repair: leaf springs and dampers suspended the rear axle, and up front a leaf spring/rod set-up offered vital articulation. Telescopic shock absorbers aided rebound and ride control. The suspension reflected 1930s developments and engineering knowledge taken from numerous sources – not least hill-climbing, agriculture, and the 'Specials' movement, therefore the handling was firm, with reasonable roll angles, a low

The full, all-weather canvas top with plastic glazed side windows was efficient and kept the winter weather out – vital for troop health and morale.

to be standardized on the central tunnel beside the gear lever. A three-speed transmission driving all four wheels (or just the rear wheels as the front drive could be locked out by choice for higher-speed cruising), which would reduce mechanical stress and fuel consumption, was offered. A two-speed transfer mechanism and

centre of gravity, and 'sporty' character. The suspension was therefore 'sporting' and not with excessive roll angles or wallow despite the large wheel travel and articulation. Oversteer was obvious in the rear-wheel drive-only selection mode, whereas with the full four-wheel-drive engaged, the handling was more neutral and had truer traction.

Of note: the Ford variant used a differing front shock-absorber mounting to the Willys type.

Being hydraulic, the brakes were of saloon-car quality. The hard-compound, all-terrain tyres offered little high-speed grip on a wet road.

The Jeep was only 52 inches (1.32m) high. The fold-flat windscreen would become a well-used feature, not least as it reduced reflection from the upright glass, a giveaway to enemy spotters. Some Jeep units even had specially tailored canvas windscreen covers to mount over the windscreen and its frame to eliminate the chance of reflection from the glass.

The tilt, or hood was made of fabric dyed as close to olive drab as possible, although some beige hoods have been cited. The canvas hood could easily be folded and its steel hoops collapsed. A hood storage locker was supplied in the cabin. The hood's material was chemically impregnated with a waterproofing compound and with an anti-mildew substance. Fire-resistance came from chemical treatment, but this had a short life when exposed to the elements.

A strong, welded-steel mounting pintle was placed between the seats to provide a mount for guns or even a rocket launcher/bazooka. Perhaps by accident, it allowed a large degree of elevation for such weapons.

Of note: after D-Day, Jeeps in Normandy and its locale were soon seen with a strange vertically mounted metal 'post' standing over five feet high from a mounting and bracing on the front bumper. This was a wire-cutting device that would cut any wires placed at head-height across a road that could decapitate the driver and occupants. This trick was a desperate late-1944 tactic deployed by some German units in France and required a swift, 'bolt-on' solution by the Allies after several Jeep crews were killed driving at high speed into such razor-wire traps

Differences

The early Willys-built Jeep had the simple, slatted-bar grill panel that was welded up from steel rods in a time-consuming and expensive process. These 'Slatties' were produced until mid-March 1942 with 25,808 being manufactured prior to the adoption of the Ford grill of pressed steel type – this being lighter, cheaper

The addition of the vertical steel wire-cutter was a vital life saving device in European and Pacific theatres. It was mounted and braced upon the front bumper and saved many Jeep occupants from their enemies sabotage habits.

Troops would often hang kit bags and their gear from the Jeep's numerous non-official attachment points.

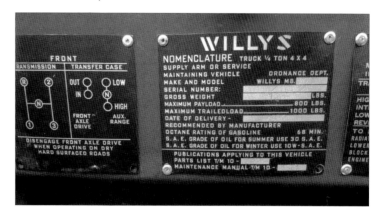

The vital 'Nomenclature' as attached to the Jeep fascia. Note the instruction to disengage the front wheel drive when driving on normal roads – to save transmission wear and fuel.

and quicker to build. The Willys and Ford 1941-produced versions would differ in several details – notably the grill, and the front chassis cross-member design in which the Ford-built Jeep used an inverted U-section shape for its main chassis front member, whereas the Willys variant used a tubular section member.

But the most obvious factor of the difference between the two types was that front grill/valance panel. It was Ford that designed the later defining, metal panel stamped front-grill design motif with nine slots – the Willys version of seven slots replacing the early-type Willys grill which was the framed, slot-and-bar grill expensively welded up.

Early slat-grill Willys Jeeps did not have the under-dashboard glovebox and shelf. The fire extinguisher was mounted in the *right-hand* footwell – as opposed to the left-hand footwell on subsequent Jeeps from mid-1942. The simpler, lightweight wheels were also replaced with stronger combat specification wheels. Ford Jeeps initially had a curved side access aperture, but the tub was soon standardized to the straight-edged cutaway.

MB-series saw the addition of a larger fuel tank to increase range (15US gal/ 56l), new side panel work to allow the mounting of spades and axes, an improved canvas roof or tilt with an extra hoop support and revised 6-volt battery. External fuel tank/can mounts were also added. By late 1942, further additions included handles on the body to help troops haul the Jeep out of mud (or snow) and small rear bumper bars mounted on the chassis ends.

Although equipped with a canvas roof that could be erected to provide some degree of weather protection, the Jeep's open-sided design allowed all weather conditions to penetrate the cabin and its occupants. A quick fix was to fit canvas, in-fill side panels into the cutaway body beside each front-seat occupant. The addition of full side panels (with plastic vision panels) and ultimately a metal, sealed hard top, would solve the issues of catching a cold or pneumonia in a Jeep.

Fuel was to be a critical issue for any landborne force. The Jeep had a 15-gallon tank, but up to late 1943, the daily amount of fuel used 'per wheeled vehicle' that the U.S. Army had based its fuel supply calculations upon, was 5 gallons a day per vehicle. This figure was a somewhat random guesstimate of fuel use in a combat zone that took little heed of differing vehicle types and their different miles-per-gallon consumption figures. It would become vital that extra fuel tanks – U.S. QMC type or British tanks, and then the popular 'jerry can' types – could all be fitted to the Jeep body to extend the vehicle's range.

By 1943, the concept of an in-theatre Jeep – repaired and rebuilt many times in the field – made the idea of a mix-and match Willys–Ford unique Jeep compilation of parts a reality. Today we have the reality of the Willys–Ford–Hotchkiss hybridized Jeep in all the required restoration parts. A cadre of expert Jeep restorers, and holders of many unique and rare original parts can be found in America and Britain. Some original parts can also be located in Europe. Sadly, many 'fakes' or pattern 'replica' parts also exist. Originality and authenticity are highly prized aspects of Jeep restoration and ownership. It is also clear that post-1946 CJ-series Jeeps have been modified to resemble original Jeeps; an expert can spot the false provenance however.

A few long-wheel-base Jeeps with extended chassis and bodies and room for eight to ten men were also produced in theatre during the Second World War.

Bantam-built official Jeep trailers were vital to adding payload and ability to the agile Jeep. Two-trailer towed in tandem was not unheard of.

101st Airborne
The essential 101st Airborne Jeep with 327 HQ 5 markings in olive drab depicted with windscreen up. Based in Wiltshire, UK, prior to D-Day and the Normandy campaign.

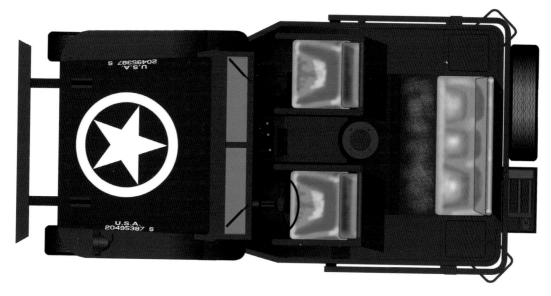

Soviet Lend-Lease
Minimal markings apart from the identifying red star.
Lighter shade of olive drab. Note the cold climate/
'Arctic' type steel hardtop with glazed sides and doors.

8th AFB Group

Pale yellow marked the airfield rescue/operations specification Jeep. Deployed East Anglia 1943-1944. Marked as 8 AF, 401 Bomber Group.

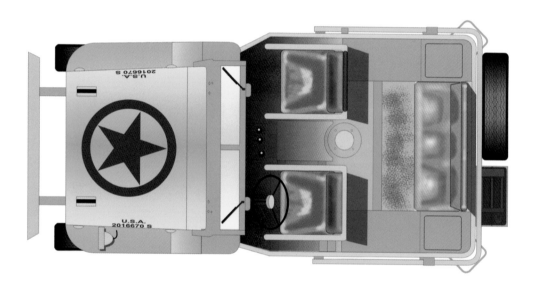

No. 4 Recce Group
Post-June 1944 2nd Reconnaissance Group
Jeep seen in olive drab with front-mounted
wire cutter as fitted in Normandy in late-1944.
Seen in lightweight 'agile' minimal equipment
specification.

U.S. Navy Jeep
Late-war U.S.N. Shore-based HQ Jeep in pale blue with yellow U.S.N. markings. Available in pale grey, and pale blue (Pacific theatre).

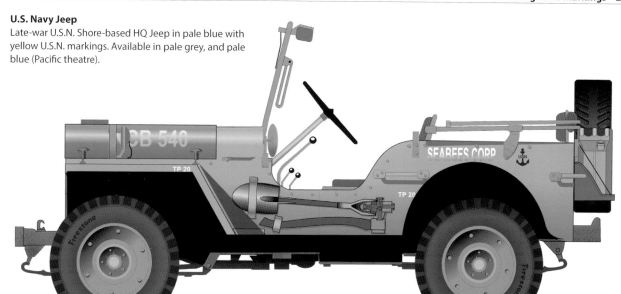

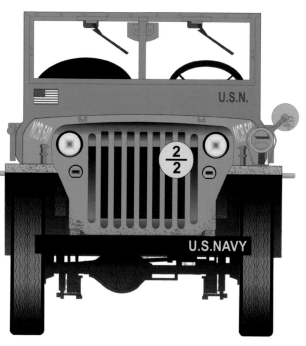

British Airborne Division
Post-June 1944 with 'Pegasus' unit markings and front-mounted spare wheel. Windscreen folded. Minimal-spec for glider deployment.

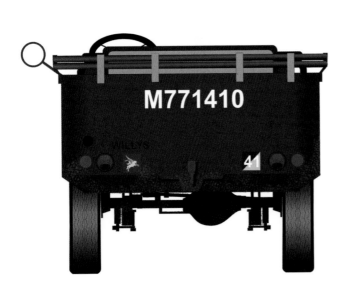

India China Div
'Weathered' ICD Jeep marked for 1944 Burma
Campaign. Canvas side panels fitted. Similar to 'Flying
Tigers' marked unit Jeeps.

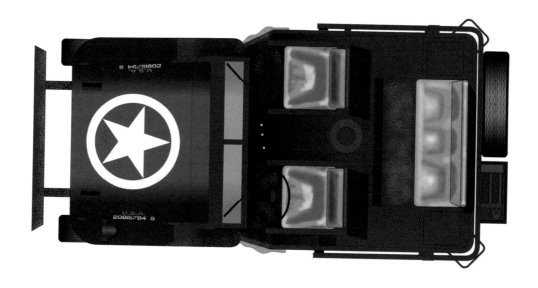

U.S. Army Armoured
1944-1945 body armoured mini-turret Jeep with heavy-calibre weapon on floor mounting. Used in Ardennes winter campaign against the German incursion. Note the front panel armament plate. One of two types of body armour 'towers' were offered. Also used by Soviet Forces.

Lond Range Desert Group (LRDG)
British LRDG North Africa Jeep 1942-1943 in Light Buff, with multi-calibre double-armament in cabin and 10 long-range fuel tanks on body. Note the radiator condenser unit and grill modifications.

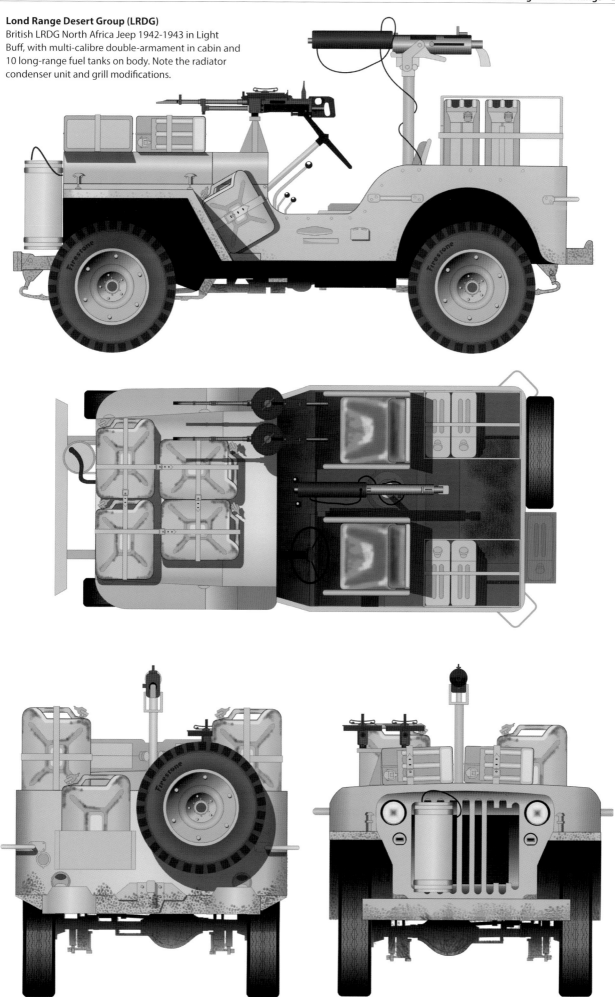

SAS JEEP
British L Detachment SAS, North Africa
1/35 Scale
Przemek Marek

This was supposed to be an easy project, an interlude between more complex ones but similar to others based on a real photo of the vehicle used by the SAS. The base kit was Tamiya #35033 upgraded with Eduard photo etched part from sets #35795. The stowage is from Tamiya Allied vehicles accessory set plus my spare's box. Despite its age the kit comes together rather nicely with no major fitting problems. It was just another inexpensive project that perhaps demanded a bit more work to be completed and is proof that even the older kits can get a new life with the addition of some extra detailing.

The camouflage net was cut from a car polishing cloth, soaked in white glue, formed to shape and painted in earthy colors with the use of airbrush.

The SAS soldier figures provided in the kit are in my opinion below the current standards so they were replaced with figures from Master Box #3598 LRDG in North Africa with no conversions..

All the jerry cans provided in the kit are too simplified and had to be replaced either by newer ones from Tamiya's set, or something from the reach contents of my box of spares.

The clothing at the front and rear of the jeep, as well as most of the straps, are made of led foil from a good wine bottle.

The Jeep as well as figures were painted with Vallejo acrylics and Windsor and Newton oils.

The base was made from a picture frame filled with a thin slice of Styrofoam covered in Vallejo acrylic groundwork paste and shaped to represent the shifting sands of the desert. In order to obtain the effect of the fine sand, the groundwork was covered in ground pastels mixed with matt acrylic medium. The dry moss is from the garden and the barbed wire was home made from copper wire of various diameters.

SAS 'Command Car'
Western Front
1/35 Scale
Brian Richardson

This is the Italeri 1/35 'Commando Car' kit built nearly out of the box. Eduard do a PE set for this kit but I opted to scratch the added detail instead. After the North African campaign British SAS operations moved to Northwest Europe and lessons learned helped improve the Jeep's fighting ability. This model represents one of those vehicles. Parachute brigades also made use of these versatile 1/4 tonners as did French, Belgian Special forces and Popskie's Private Army. The original Italeri kit was first issued in 1976 with an extra sprue added for the 'Command Car' in 1980 so for its age it still builds up into a respectable model.

Most period photos show the front grill bars removed leaving only the two centres and some were fitted with stays supporting the front mud guards, these were added with 0.4mm copper wire. A small Red Cross decal was sourced from a spare sheet as no decals are proved with the kit and most vehicles seemed to carry a first aid kit.

The only real negative would the Italeri brand name moulded under the floor pan and the soldier figure is probably best left in the spares box.

The other additions include some resin packs, bed rolls and ammo liners to replace the kit parts. Masking tape handles were added to each K gun's drum magazine.

The kit wheels only required valve stems to be added from stretched sprue and the exhaust pipe is drilled out.

As the standard windscreen was removed from these Jeeps the brackets were also removed leaving holes in the body work and these were drilled out. Tamiya acrylics, enamels, oils and chalk pastels took care of the painting and weathering. Finally a 2B pencil was applied to high wear areas and the weapons for that bare metal look.

The plus features would have to be the MG's and the brand Firestone moulded into the tyre side walls. The other nice touch is the inclusion of clear head light lenses, most other kits at the time were solid. The headlights have had thin copper wiring added along with handles made from a thin aluminium strip cut from left over food containers.

WILLY'S MB
Italian Campaign, 1944
1/35 Scale
Przemek Marek

The inspiration for the project was a photograph depicting an artillery forward observer's Willys MB of the 151st Field Artillery Regiment, 34th Division, seen on the Cassino front in Italy on 17 January 1944. Having constructed several Jeeps I was left with a substantial spare's box. This included pricey front wheels with chains from Czech company Black Dog. In order to make good use of them I decided to wrap this next project around these wheels with the minimum addition of other aftermarket parts, just enough to drain my spares box. A dated Tamiya #35033 was the kit of choice: obsolete by today's standards and although inferior to the Tamiya #35219 it was half the price. Overall the outcome may provide bait for more discerning modellers but it was a fun build and great satisfaction bringing the old photograph into three dimension with minimal expense.

Construction started from the retro fitting of the missing radiator grill bars. Then the chassis was fitted and glued to the frame and suspension leaf springs, after they were cleaned of a fair amount of flash.

As the windscreen was missing completely from this kit, I kept one from the SK Model #11400 version of the Jeep once produced by Heller. The windscreen is the only decent part of that kit.

Figures are from Miniart #35047 US Jeep Crew set, converted slightly to be as close a representation of the men in the photograph as possible. While the standing figure was modified only slightly, the radio operator went through major surgery. The headphones were scratch built and the ranks, as well as unit badges of the 34th US Infantry Division, were hand painted.

The only after market addition purchased specifically for this project was a rear antenna and its mount which comes from Aber #R-25.

The M1A1 carbine and its holder come from Tamiya #35219. It was masked by lead foil from a wine bottle to represent a half tent used for cover. Then some leftover Eduard photo etched parts were added along with copper wire to increase the detail.

The seats are very basic so new ones were made from wire and bits of styrene. The rear also has a piece of Evergreen rod, bent into shape with the help of the hair dryer.

The SCR 600 radio set was built entirely from styrene, wire and the parts of frames from spare photo etched parts.

The reel stand and its mountings were made from scratch from the frames of the PE parts and Evergreen styrene rods of a suitable diameter.

After priming with Vallejo primer (German grey) the kit was sprayed with gradually lighter coats of olive drab from the range of Vallejo acrylics. When dry, the paintwork was washed with Windsor and Newton oils using the 'paint dot' technique to break the monotony of the olive drab camouflage. Finally weathering was achieved with ground pastels mixed with matt acrylic medium and water.

WILLY'S MB

5th Armoured Division, Normandy, summer 1944

1/35 Scale

Brian Richardson

Tamiya's 1997 release #35219 Willy's MB JEEP kit builds into an accurate replica of this classic 1/4 ton 4X4 general purpose vehicle. The kit comes with a well-moulded, single-driver figure and optional parts are included for a wire cutter, tow bar and pedestal mounted 1919 .30cal MG and five decal options give the modeller plenty of choice. This model represents a vehicle with Service Company No. 4, 95th Armoured Field Artillery Battalion, 5th Armoured Division.

As good as the Tamiya kit is there are quite a few rivets, press studs and bolts missing but armed with a few clear photos of restored vehicles these can easily be added with salami-sliced stretched sprue.

The bonnet/windscreen latches are also missing and I made these from copper wire and 0.5mm brass tube. The windscreen wiper motors and black out light need some cable so a short length of 0.32mm copper was added around the frame and a pair of left over PE stays replaced the kit parts for a more realistic scale appearance.

No brake or clutch pedals are provided and these were fashioned from thin card and rod. I've also removed the rifle from part B9 and chiselled out the scabbard as well as adding straps to the shovel and axe. A new jerry can and tub replaced the solid kit part and a valve stem added to each road wheel.

The driver's mirror is rather simplified so a new arm was made from tube, wire and the kit mirror. Retaining chains were added to the folding frames and windscreen attachment points.

I've mixed my own Olive Drab from Tamiya XF-62 and XF-60 Dark Yellow followed with many enamel/oil washes. I chose to do decal option A and the kit's decals work well with Mr Softer and a little heat from a hair dryer. Humbrol Matt Coat sealed everything with a little graphite from a 6B pencil rubbed over high-wear areas to simulate bare steel.

The Jeep is a modellers' favourite and regularly appears in modelling magazines and web sites. A global Jeep enthusiasm exists. Modellers study the Jeep in all its variations and details. 1957 saw the first true mass production Jeep/ ¼ Ton Truck model tooled and launched by Monogram at 1/35 scale. In 1973 Monogram launched a Jeep kit with the addition of the 37mm M3 anti-tank gun/trailer. The key 1970s, 1990s, 2000s Jeep / ¼ Ton Truck model manufacturers include: Tamiya, Airfix, Hasegawa, Italeri / Testors, Hobbystar, Dragon, Miniart, Bronco, Pte. Arsenal: Monogram, Heller and Revell made earlier toolings in the 1970s for their Jeep models respectively. Science Treasury, and Popye, also released licensed mouldings. The S- Model (China) brand has issued a 2017 tooling. Recent re-issues and sets have seen new boxes and some new toolings amid various sub-licensing and re-issues of mouldings – as has been the case since the 1970s.

For trademark and licensing reasons, many kit model manufacturers avoid reference to the 'Jeep' trademark for legal reasons and market their products as ¼ Ton Truck'.

Typical manufacturer depictions include: 101st Airborne, British 6th Airborne Division, D-Day, Ardennes Campaign, Recce Groups, Divisional Headquarters, U.S. 1st Infantry Division. LRDP/SAS and SAS Northern Europe.

The first plastic Jeep models emerged in the 1950s and several 1960s–1970s–1980s toolings have been released and re-released under various licences. This can cause reductions in quality of moulding and reproductions of detail. Because the Jeep is a flat-side design, any panting, dimpling and moulding issues can be more obvious in the body panels than they might be on a more complex, more curved moulding. Modellers are advised to research the age of a kit's manufacturing origins and any sub-licensing of toolings in order to maximise the quality of their Jeep model building. Recent issues from **Airfix** (2004, 2014), Tamiya and Hasegawa represent more contemporary toolings of the 1990s and 2000s, but other kits are available.

DML as **Dragon** manufacture a high quality Jeep moulding that has also been used as a base by licencees. An initial issue with the grill moulding has been addressed in more recent toolings of 2012 onwards. Dragon has also produced the 1/6 scale Jeep, and the rare armoured version which is ideal for modification by the modeller. A recent 1/35 scale LRDG/SAS release has excellent detailing and armament options.

Popular scales for the Jeep are 1/35, 1/48, and 1/72.

Dragon's Armour ¼ Ton 4x4 Truck with Bazookas. . The decal options for this are US Army 9th Infantry Division, 60th Infantry Regiment in the Battle for the Ardennes, Belgium 1945.

The light blue writing/ marking on this Jeep is noteworthy becasue early Jeeps used pale blue and not white lettering.

Tamiya's first Jeep kit was release as early as 1972: In 1997, kit reference 1/35 219 was a new tooling: the current Tamiya 1/48 kit is of the usual high quality we expect from Tamiya (and branded as a Jeep, by arrangement) and this Jeep kit is noteworthy for having separate body tub side panels (a bit like the Jeep itself) whereas Hasegawa's body tub is one-piece moulded. The forensically detailed Tamiya kit also correctly mounts the windscreen wipers upon the steel windscreen frame's header rail – not on the glass. Modeller's should note that in early 1945, new vacuum-operated windshield-wiper kits were available and could be retro-fitted to earlier Jeeps and can be a hybrid fitment to a model. Tamiya also offers authentic two-piece wheels.

However, the recent **Hasegawa** (first tooling released in in 1973) kit features a more detailed engine in comparison to much earlier (but not the recent) Tamiya kits. Indeed, Hasegawa have been making a Jeep model for decades – across several toolings at 1/72 scale. From the 1970s through to the 1990s and beyond, the

This British SAS Jeep was built by Maurice Monteiro. The build consists of the Tamiya base and the Swash Design SAS upgrade set as the conversion. The Tamiya kit is straightforward and a pleasure to build. The Swash design is essential if you want to build a fairly accurate version. The conversion set consists of resin and brass photo-etch. The two figures are included in the set as well.

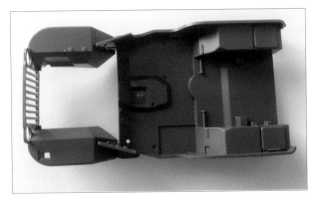

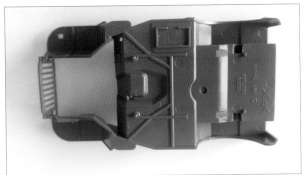

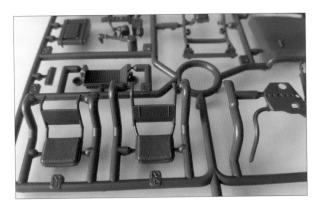

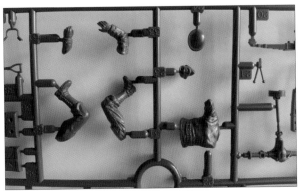

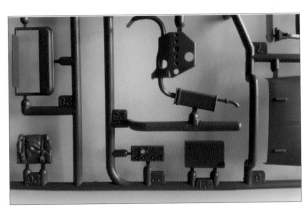

Established in 2004 the **Bronco** Mould & Plastic Company's Jeep models are in 1/35 scale and offer three variations. The 1942 Ford production GPW ¼ ton Utlity Truck with a 10-CWT trailer and three-man airborne crew. This kit's decal options are limited to the 82nd Airborne Division, Normandy, 1944. The kit is praised for its detail and high-quality mouldings. It is recommended for experienced modellers as there is a complex breakdown of some delicate parts. Their second offering is also of the Ford model utility truck this time with a 37mm anti-tank gun M3A1. The M3's decals are US Army, as are the Jeeps, although for the latter there is a choice of unit markings and theatres of operation: 3rd Battalion, 1 Armoured Regiment, Sidi Bou Zid 1943; Anti-tank Company, 60th Infantry Regiment, North Africa 1942; 6th Infantry Regiment, US 1st Armoured Division, Annunziata landin 1944, Anti-tank Company, 7th and 16th Infantry regiments. A very tricky part of this build is the gun: it's amazing but comes at a price as there are many small parts that need extreme care in both removing from the sprues and during assembly, with a number of the miniature sub-assemblies being designed to be movable after assembly. The third kit is titled: British Airborne Troops Riding in ¼ ton Truck & Trailer and the decals are all British Army 1st and 6th Airborne divisions, North West Europe 1944. This kit does not deviate from the attention to detail and quality of the others and again calls for an experienced modeller because of the many fine parts.

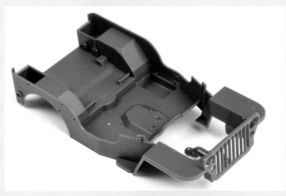

These sprues are from the US GPW ¼ ton Utlity Truck with 10-CWT trailer and three-man airborne crew kit.

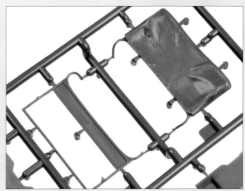

This Jeep depicts the windscreen and frame folded down – which was the default setting for many Jeeps in many theatres of war.

company has offered a series of well-detailed Jeep and Jeep-trailer kits also featuring a gun.

The **Airfix** Jeeps have not only been of good quality, they have offered numerous variations including airborne, D-Day, ambulance and other options. A 2014 new tooling with numerous options has provided fresh impetus to the Airfix rendition of the Jeep which has been well received by modellers.

Italeri, **Hobbystar** and Dragon, provide kits of a quality relevant to the serious modeller, and of course, the hybridisation of a cross-kit variant is of appeal to the modeller. Individual decals from dedicated decal suppliers are also highly recommended.

Whichever the kit, there are certain specific issues that apply to modelling the Jeep, and these can cause

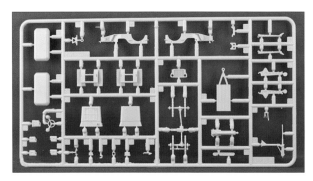
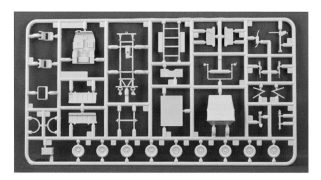

headaches but also great satisfaction, for the advanced-level modeller.

Weathering: This is a model making area of recent focus that is very appropriate to the Jeep. Of note, the North Africa Desert theatre Jeeps suffered severe weathering from sand blasting and use. Such Jeeps need to look used, well-worn and show their modifications, maintenance issues and equipment variations.

Jeeps used in the India/Burma/China theatres and the Pacific campaign are also likely to be realistic in showing tropical weathering and corrosion. Mud being particularly appropriate.

Another specific issue for the Jeep modeller is the variety of armament configurations that were fitted to the Jeep. Careful research will allow the modeller to depict an array of light, medium, and heavier calibre armament – up to anti-tank equipment and heavy calibre machine guns (.50 calibre). The distinct types of armour plating added to the Jeep also allow great personal expression in the Jeep model.

The early Jeeps have been popularly designated Very Early Production (VEP) and contained a number of differing specifications and consequent variations in primer, paint, chassis and details. For example VEP Slat Grill Jeeps used a black primer or a mix of black or zinc-chromate. So the modeller needs to carefully research the date of production of such Jeeps and also consider the wide opportunities offered to the modeller from depicting in-service, local, 'one-off'

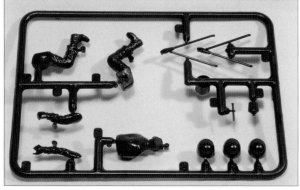

Images courtesy of Brian Robinson.

Images courtesy of Brian Robinson.

Italeri has three 1/24 scale Second World War Jeep kits: the stand-alone Jeep with six decal options; the 'utility' jeep with M2 machine gun which has decal options for four versions and an ARMA Dei Carabinieri. In its 1/35 scale range Italeri offers modellers four jeep kits that have been reboxed and released over the past forty-odd years. The Willys Jeep with trailer and three figures is available in four decal options, two are US Marine Corps (Iwo Jima and Guam) and two are US Army (Monte Cassino and Normandy). The Commando Car includes one figure, although they usually had a crew of two, and includes five machine guns and additional fuel tanks. The Ambulance Jeep has two decal options and the Utility Truck, which is based on Revell's Willy's Jeep, has wire cutters, an M2 machine gun and four decal options. Italeri also produces a 1/72 fast-assembly kit for wargaming. A few of these product kits showed as out of stock on Itaerli's website although second-hand and surplus stock may still be available from suppliers and end users. A closer look at the moulding of their kits reveals a few sink marks that will need to be filled before construction but genrally that the detail is crisp. Although modellers agree that there are kits available now that rival Italeri, the quality of the sprues and the fit build up into a very decent model, one that stands up to the likes of Tamiya, at a very competitive price.

Red Cross marked Ambulance Jeep modelled with heavy weathering to match the mud of late 1944 in France and Belgium.

variations. Again, North African, Soviet, airborne and Ardennes campaign Jeeps offer great scope for such interpretations.

Other VEP anomalies relate to chassis paint, body tub primer, WILLYS stamps on slat grille and windscreen scuttle panels, and engine paint colours. For example, Jeeps had their engine bays painted in a series of colours and their engine blocks were painted in differing colours according to manufacture and date. Ford engines in early 1942 were painted grey (code M4984-G) from chassis No 26207, until grey (code M1788-G) superseded it, itself superseded by M1788-H after late September 1942.

Details such as the fitting of an engine bay-mounted grease gun, which was fitted across Ford and Willys Jeeps, Willys depending on which Ford Factory manufactured the Jeep from late 1943 or early 1944 depending on manufacturing location, also add to the modellers debate.

The forensic modeller might also note the differing colour of the wooden blocks fitted to the bonnet/hood to support the windscreen and frame when folded down. Similarly, the variations on the shades of Olive Drab are to be noted – the British use of such colour being a darker shade at one period. Aspects such a tyre pressure (TP), markings and those of battalion, regiment or unit, need careful research and rendition.

Of interest to is that there were differing specifications to early Ford production Jeeps and differing codes and stamps on chassis frames and components. Clearly, sourcing components from different factories and suppliers, explains such anomalies, but they are worth noting for the restorer and the model maker.

During the first months of production, various different types and colours of primer were used on the Jeep's body, grill and parts – built at the respective factories; depicting weathering to such examples as modelled, requires careful research.

In the modelling world, the Jeep represents a true highlight and one of the greatest opportunities for interpretation. The depiction of the Second World War Jeep also permits memorial and tribute to be made to those men that used the Jeep in the circumstances of conflict – a war and an outcome that the Jeep, without doubt, influenced.

OTHER KIT MANUFACTURERS

Revell makes two sets available to modellers: a 1/35 scale M34 Tactical Truck and Jeep and a Morris Truck & 17pdr Gun & Jeep. Revell's stand-along Jeep is a Utlity vehicle with four decal options. Academy has a 1/72 scale Second World War three-piece ground vehicle set available which includes a Willys Jeep. MisterCraft does a ¼ Ton Truck 'Willys' in 1/72 scale. Plus Models have three jeeps available all in 1/35 scale: Pattond's Jeep, See Bee Jeep and a Jeep M38. Bilek is the only other manufacturer to offer an armoured Jeep, this one in 1/35 scale. The Czech resin models manufacturer Black Dog has a few Jeeps in its collection, mostly a variation on the same theme across three scales: 1/35, 1/48 and 1/72. This is the famous Stirling SAS Jeep in North Africa, although a 1944 European Jeep is also available. A combo kit with a Chevrolet. They do a 1/48 scale Jeep with rocket launcher conversion set and Jeep accessories. A 1/72 and a 1/35 scale US ¼ ton Truck and Trailer are available from Heller: they have 55 and 107 parts respectively. The Heller kits are very reasonable priced, in the same affordable range as Airfix.

Key modelling essentials checklist:
There are many points to note for the Jeep modeller, some of them are cited here:

◊ Willys logo stamped into the windscreen base support panel as appropriate.
◊ Body panel details appropriate to Jeep variant.
◊ Under-floor body pressings and panels variations.
◊ Slat grill and welded bar grill, front panel: as relevant.
◊ Bumper bars as appropriate.
◊ Front longeron/cross member shapes as per variant.
◊ Cabin details and seat pads and backs.
◊ Fire extinguisher location.
◊ First Aid kit location.
◊ Dashboard /glovebox configuration.
◊ Windscreen covers for beach assault Jeeps.
◊ Fold-back Ford-type headlamps.
◊ Side straps, canvas, seating and trims.
◊ Gun racks to dashboard – leather or steel.
◊ Tyre tread, type, size.
◊ Stretcher/Litter fittings.
◊ Engine as fitted to respective Marks/variants.
◊ Engine block paint colours.
◊ Engine pulleys and ancilliaries.
◊ Engine bay colour.
◊ Paint scheme and markings (Example: Unit sign and serial number. Formation sign. Convoy sign. White star. Stars to side panels. Gas detection patch. Jeep chassis number registration. Tyre pressure markings. Dimensions and weights markings).
◊ Armament and armour.
◊ Pintle and floor pan details.
◊ Headlamp lenses.
◊ Towing eyes, attachment points.
◊ Correct depiction of crew.
◊ After-market model accessories and sets include ambulance conversion, modified armament, snow chains and storage, tyre and wheel variations, decal options. Photo-etching improvements.

Classic Jeep pose – the canvas 'tilt' hood and the enclosed all-weather version are compared.

Running with rear-side panels but without the doors gave some degree of weather protection yet retained the vital quick access from the two front seats.

Various military units produced their own modified and tweaked Jeeps.

The Jeep also had a rather unfortunate flaw in one specific aspect of its design. This related to the fact that under severe braking from high speed, the Jeep had a propensity to veer to one side (the left-hand driver's or left side). Young Jeep drivers could not understand this and much investigation went on to discover the cause. This lay within the way the worm and roller steering mechanism was mounted, and its use of bell cranks. The associated locating rods were of unequal length, the cranks mounted not on a sub-frame but onto the front axle. Under heavy braking load, the axle tended to move about itself – to rotate – and this combined with the effect of the bell crank actuators and the leaf spring, created a torque-twist reaction in the steering and axle gear. The left-hand side of the mechanism was under compression load and the right-hand side under opposing tension load. This resulted in a 'pull' to the left under severe retardation.

By early 1943, a 'fix' was found via the fitting or a torque spring rod. Moving the bell crank mount from the axle mount to a cross member would also reduce the effect. But Jeep drivers knew that braking and steering at high speed were not without risk.

Why was the Jeep so narrow? The answer was that its creators knew that it would have to fit into military transport vehicles for transportation – by ground, sea and air. Remember, a Jeep could fit into a 1930s military air transport machine and a glider such as the American-designed and -built Waco, or the British Horsa. Strapped to a shock-load absorbing pallet, the Jeep could also be dropped by parachute directly into the theatre of operations. And if a Jeep snapped a leaf spring on landing, it could be replaced in a short time.

Guns, automatic weapons, mortars, panniers, stretchers, fire hoses, winches, rail-wheels, in fact almost anything

Specifications
Willys MB *circa* 1943

Body/Chassis: Steel-ladder type with differences in some section shapes according to manufacturer
Lightweight external body tub and panels in steel
Engine: Willys model 441, or, 442 'Go-Devil' 4 cylinder in-line, side-valve, L-head, water-cooled petrol engine
Cubic capacity: 2,199cc (2.2l)
Horsepower: 60bhp at 4,000rpm
Torque: 105lb/ft (142Nm)
Carburettor: Carter Type WO-539S
Transmission: Borg & Beck Type 11123 single dry-plate clutch. 3 forward speeds. 1 rear speed. Spicer axle/differential units
Selectable four-wheel drive/two-wheel (rear) drive. PTO off main driveshaft
Gear ratios: First 2.665 / Second 1.564 / Third 3.554 / Reverse 3.554
High Range: 13.005 / 7.632 / 4.880 / Reverse 17.344
Low Range: 25.573 / 15.036 / 9.614 / Reverse 34.167
Suspension: Semi-elliptic leaf springs all-round with telescopic dampers/shock absorbers. Note the differences in Willys, and Ford front shock-absorber mountings
Brakes: Four-wheel hydraulic. Mechanical parking brake on transfer case output
Electrical System: 6 volt. (Note: adjustable generator bracket permits slackening of fan belt)
Dimensions:
Track: 49¼in (1.25m) front and rear
Wheelbase: 80in (2.03m)
Total length: 131in (3.33m)
Overall width: 52in (1.32m)
Height (with windscreen folded): 52in (1.32m)
Dry weight: 2,337lb (1,92kg)

(including a rocket launcher) could be mounted on, to, or in a Jeep. An armoured Jeep was less nimble but offered real protection to its occupants.

Built during the war by Ford, and by Willys, over 639,245 wartime Jeeps were manufactured as the world's first large-volume manufacture four-wheel-drive vehicle.

Cpl. Alyce Dixon (right) poses with members of the 6888th Central Postal Directory Battalion. The only African-American Women's Army Corps unit to serve in Europe during the Second World War. The battalion was responsible for clearing a massive backlog of mail in England and then France. Their jobs were crucial to morale at the front. (Photo: US Army Medical Corps)

The wooden blocks on the bonnet stop the windscreen glass from touching the bonnet when running folded-down. Note the simple-to-fix exposed front leaf springs and chassis details.

A Jeep could be loaded up with enough kit to let its occupants roam for days without re-supply. Art work was often applied in-the-field – as seen here.

This later Ford-type with full-weather kit shows just how versatile the design was. This was a more comfortable Jeep.

Production December 1941–August 1945	
Bantam-built (1940):	2,675
Willys-built:	361,349
Ford-built:	277,896
Total:	639,245

(Note: Between 1942 and 1945, Jeep bodies were built by American Central Manufacturing Corporation of Connersville, Indiana.)

During the Second World War, an amphibious GPA Jeep known as the 'Seep' was constructed – over 10,000 were constructed in a short lifespan. Perhaps inspired by the famous DUKW 'Duck', the Seep was too heavy with little freeboard and shipped a lot of water in even light seas. Yet it provided vital support in the invasion of Italy in 1943. Some Seeps found their way to the USSR, and also saw service in France and on the Rhine-crossing campaign in late 1944.

The interior of this Jeep shows the fuel tank under the driver's seat before it curved down underneath, and the 'hip' pads added beside each front seat to stop occupants bashing their hip bones against the side-panel on rough roads – a small but vital Jeep detail.

In Service and in Action

Jeep went to war quickly. Firstly, in 1941 it was shipped to Britain under the Lend-Lease Act, then onward to the USSR from June 1941 when several thousand early models were shipped across the Atlantic. One of the earliest U.S. outfits that would benefit from the availability of a vehicle like the Jeep before the United States of America entered the war would be the Special Army Observer Group which became operational in May 1941. As American involvement in the war developed (post-December 1941), so too did the Jeep and then came the vital areas of the Second World War in which the Jeep contributed to the outcome – the Pacific campaign of Oceania and Asia, and the North African and Italian theatres prior to Jeep's role in the D-Day invasion and the race across France and over the Rhine into Germany. As 1942 dawned and America's war commitments expanded, Jeeps went everywhere. The term 'Jeep Platoon' soon came to frame the type's service contribution. Jeeps served in several Canadian units including the Canadian Armoured Division and the Royal Canadian Air Force, Tactical Air Force in Normandy in late 1944.

The Airborne Division and D-Day Jeeps are well known and well represented in current Jeep history and in restorations and modelling, but Pacific region and Western Desert Jeep operations should not be overlooked – notably the Burma, China, and non-LRDG applications respectively.

Jeep enthusiasts will have their own personal preferences and prejudices as to which theatre was the most important, but we can surely cite all the regions of warfare and the vital contribution of the genius of the Jeep to them as critical to the outcome.

The key Jeep theatres of contribution (in order of wartime chronology) were:

Domestic U.S. service requirements
Britain
USSR
North Africa
Italy
India/Burma/China
Pacific
D-Day: France/Low Countries/Germany

From 1941, the British Army used early-model BRC, Willys, (and then Ford Jeeps) to great effect in the North African campaign and in the Long Range Desert Group (forerunner to the Special Air Service/ SAS) activities. These Jeeps were adapted to carry long-range fuel, rations and armament supplies and their own spares. Keeping sand out of the carburettor and the oil and fuel was vital to keeping the engines running. A radiator condenser was fitted to aid cooling in the high ambient operating temperatures, Even Scottish and Canadian regiments were to become Jeep-mounted. The Argyll and Sutherland Highlanders, part of the 4th Canadian Armoured Division, II Canadian Corps, made rapid advances across Normandy in Jeeps in July 1944. By 1945, Royal Air Force-marked Jeeps (RAF

Top: A Waco glider awaits an aerial-land hook up and tow-launch as the C-47 is talked-in for the pick-up by a Jeep-mounted control team. Note the large radio set behind the driver, and the 20ft radio mast on the bumper. (Photo: USAAC/DoD).

Above: Ford Nomenclature. Note the 65mph maximum permissible speed.

roundel on bonnet) were penetrating deep into Germany alongside those of the British Army and U.S. forces.

In the push across North Africa after the Allied invasion in November 1942 American troops made fast gains by Jeep. The British and Americans pushed General Rommel and his Afrika Korps back and Jeeps helped the pace. Jeeps were parachuted to Italian partisans in 1943 and by 1943 mobilized the U.S. Fifth Army as it headed northward through Italy in a long and bloody campaign to rebut the well-embedded German forces under the redoubtable Field Marshal A. Kesselring. French troops entered Tunis in Jeeps as early as 1943; the Jeep had allowed them to move at speed in this part of the desert campaign that turned the tide against the Germans.

The Royal Indian Army Corps received Jeeps, as did British troops in Burma and Chinese forces fighting the Japanese. In that year, Chinese troops were Ford GP Jeep-mounted in the China–Burma campaign (Flying Tigers Squadron). British MB Jeeps in Burma were sealed with partial tarpaulin tilt and canvas doors, but with open sides to allow airflow in the heat.

The Jeep's role in Pacific theatre service is one of its core contributions as the Americans fought their away, island by island across the Pacific amid some of the toughest land (and sea) battles of the Second World War. The U.S. Marine divisions relied upon the Jeep as they battled their way from the Solomon Islands and vital Guadalcanal then north to Okinawa. To the south, Australian forces relied on the Jeep in the sodden jungles of New Guinea.

Jeeps were air-dropped with the Allied airborne divisions in Operation Market Garden on 17 September 1944. Anti-tank guns were towed behind many of these Jeeps. Armored Jeeps and Jeeps with snowplows fitted, served in the Ardennes campaign, the Battle of the Bulge, after the German offensive of December 1944. General Patton was Jeep-mounted in this vital arena. Hand-applied winter camouflage schemes were created for the armoured Jeeps in this sector.

The U.S. Army Air Corps and U.S. Army Air Force used Jeeps for a wide variety of purposes in numerous liveries. Even the Germans used Jeeps: captured Jeeps were used, notably in disguise behind Allied lines in the Ardennes offensive of late 1944. At one stage 57 German Jeeps, containing some English-speaking German commandos, caused mayhem, even penetrating behind the lines. Acts of sabotage by the disguised Germans was achieved, including the misdirecting of American troops, such as the 15th Infantry Regiment,

In 1945 Jeep's were used to mobilise the U.S. administration of the Ibaraki Military Government Team in Japan and this example depicts such markings.

Above: With a metal rifle holder on the fascia and leather weapon holder mounted externally, this Jeep has plenty of hand-held fire power. Note the manually-operated windscreen wipers on the header rail.

Left: Even wartime Chaplains used Jeeps – as marked. A Jeep line up at the Military Vehicle Trust (MVT) Oxfordshire and a Cotswold branch event. (Photo: W.K.)

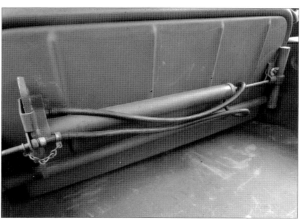

A T/5 Medical Technician of the 483rd Medical Collecting Company cleans his jeep in a rain puddle. Note the modified front wing/fender parts and special markings. 23 February 1945. (Photo: US National Archives)

Hidden under the folding rear seat of the Jeep was the air pump! A novel design solution. The greaser pump was mounted under the bonnet.

This Royal Air Force marked Jeep display extra lamp on the front wing, correctly mounted rope on the bumper bar and of note, a leather cover over the blade of the shovel – a detail for the modeller too revel in.

A minimally-equipped RAF marked Jeep at speed. Note external mounting of fire extinguisher. The earlier U.S. spec mounting of the extinguisher was to the left, or the right side of the cabin footwell.

An interesting pair of Ford (left) and Willys (right) Jeeps depicting differing specifications and appearances.

Second World War Jeep Variants

The 8th Air Force based in East Anglia used Jeeps as airfield operations and rescue vehicles. This one is from the 401st Bomber Group and marked 'Bowman's Buzzards'. Fire equipment is mounted on the right-hand side.

Jeeps served in all departments of the military; they also served the coast guard, fire services, military police, as staff cars, ambulances, Red Cross vehicles, and out in the Pacific islands, they were used by various units and groups associated not just with U.S. forces, but also the former colonial powers that had, prior to the war, overseen the region. Australians also took the Jeep to their hearts. Special equipment, numerous official and non-official paint and camouflage schemes were applied in the field to Jeeps – as were many local modifications and additions. Of often ignored significance were the gas detection patches fixed to the right side of the upper rear of the bonnet – near the occupants.

Instantaneous recognition of gas attack was vital and yet not easy as a Jeep sped along. These chemical reaction patches solved the problem.

The Jeep as an agile, high-speed personnel carrier: This was the Jeep's de facto transport role. A driver, three passengers on seats and some room for hand-carried cargo, still allowed the Jeep to make a dash for it over tarmac or non-surfaced terrain. Here was the true multi-purpose Jeep as used by soldiers from privates to generals. Adding a fourth crew member became less common in the latter stages of World War Two.

The radio Jeep: Nearly all Jeeps were equipped with medium- and short-range radios. But the rear cabin cargo bay could accommodate a larger, more sophisticated long-range radio and its generator. Special aerial mounts and wiring kits were soon devised. The U.S. Corps of Signals also mounted revolving cable drums on Jeeps in order to lay communications cables.

The scout/reconnaissance Jeep: These were the essential tasks of the most agile Jeeps and their drivers. A highly capable radio set was fitted, as was a Browning machine gun mounted on the between-the-seats pintle mount. Rarely was a bonnet-mounted heavier-calibre machine gun fitted – with the operator occupying the passenger seat, or standing. Extra fuel tanks (jerry cans), ammunition racks, and a folded canvas tilt, were standardized items. A third crewmember could sit sideways in the rear among the extra supplies and kit required for the role.

The armed and armored assault/anti-tank Jeep: The agility of the Jeep, its small scale, and its off-road behaviour made it an excellent 'tank-buster' that could fire a single or twin bazooka from the centre mount over reasonable range. The key was the Jeep's ability to manouevre into a tank-destroying position faster than a tank could react. If the Jeep could get close enough, it could deliver its ordnance.

Beyond the rifles or light machine guns used by its occupants, arming the Jeep was obvious – machine guns, rockets, mortars, howitzers, all could be bolted to a Jeep. The Smart Inc. company built a Jeep with an armoured engine bay and windscreen, but weight was the challenge in retaining performance.

The need for an anti-tank role led to the fitting of armoured sheets as side and nose plates in the field – to various designs and ideas, but soon standardized as a vertical 'conning-tower'-type armoured sheet over the crew area of the Jeep – thick enough to ward off pistol, rifle, and light machine-gun bullets but unlikely to resist a direct hit from heavier-calibre armament. Two types of armoured cab 'towers' were built for these Jeeps –full height and half height beneath a centre pintle-mounted machine gun. Notably useful in the 1944 Ardennes campaign and in Soviet hands, local U.S. units in the Ardennes campaign, retro-fitted their own self-designed armour kits of steel plates on the bonnet, tub sides, and fitted armoured glass. A Jeep could be stopped by a bullet through the radiator, so an armoured steel plate mounted on the bumper bar could protect the radiator – but reduced cooling effect airflow through it – hardly likely to be an issue in the Belgian winter of 1944/5.

U.S. forces deployed armoured-cab Jeeps with rocket-firing armament fitted via 12 projectiles fitted in banks. The .50-calibre (12.7mm) machine gun was the heaviest machine gun fitted on the Jeep. The U.S. Marine Corps fitted 28 M8A2 rockets to the Jeep via a rear-mounted rocket launcher attached to a bolt-on frame. An experiment with the larger, tripod-mounted, 4.5-inch rocket launcher proved the Jeep's adaptability. High-calibre guns, even U.S.N. Mk 21/ Mk 27 3-inch guns were fitted, but the problem of securely mounting large-calibre equipment onto the Jeep chassis without twisting or breaking it soon arose. Fitting 5-inch guns was also tried by the U.S. Cavalry Board. Mounting a mortar on a Jeep was also undertaken – up to 110mm. A special mounting of a ground-to-vehicle device and changes required to the rear of the vehicle proved

Heavy-calibre armament fitted to the Jeep's central, pintle mount on the cabin floor. This fitting required the windscreen frame to be removed and bracing tripod fitted. (Photo: DoD)

time-consuming. (See British Long Range Desert Group assault Jeep.)

The central pintle mount meant that a good amount of vertical elevation was available to weapons mounted upon it – notably machine guns – giving the Jeep anti-aircraft capability.

A handful of six-wheeled, extended-chassis BRC Jeeps were built by the U.S. Army Tank Destroyer Command as an experiment in creating a heavily armed troop-carrier armed with 37mm anti-tank guns. Six of this Jeep-Carriage Motor 37mm Gun Transport were built in 1943, and an armoured version also considered, but developments in armoured car design rendered the prototypes redundant.

The ambulance Jeep: Factory-designed and field-built stretcher/litter configurations were fitted to the Jeep. These might carry one stretcher across the rear cabin, or two longitudinally, but an official modification kit created a three-stretcher steel-welded support frame that rather precariously had a 3-foot front overhang. Stretchers could be mounted above the Jeep on a special frame; a sort of roll-bar/roof rack was also fitted, which allowed two stretcher litters to be mounted above the cab. Stretchers could also be mounted on external rails beyond the edges of each side of the body. A Jeep could carry a full complement of a doctor's equipment and with an improvised operating table across the bonnet or rear tub, urgent life-saving operations could be carried out in the field. A British idea was the extension of the roof to provide extra room for carrying under cover two rear-mounted stretchers.

Medical personnel used stretcher-equipped 'Litter' Jeeps in medical battalions as well as other units such as the 70th Tank Battalion. Medics in Jeeps often worked together with medics from various units: the Medical Detachment, 254th Infantry Regiment, 63rd Infantry Division, and the 2nd Auxiliary Surgical Group teams in Italy being well-known examples.

The meteo Jeep: The Jeeps used by the meteorologists were fitted with antennae of up to 20 feet in height. Weather-sensing equipment including a barometer and pressure sensors were fitted, as was a powerful long-range radio and its associated generator in the rear part of the Jeep cabin cargo tub.

The amphibious Jeep: The first amphibious Jeeps were normal Jeeps that had been sealed up in vital under-bonnet mechanical and electrical zones and body

Reconnaissance (R2) unit Jeep with Normandy-spec wire-cutter and full post-D-Day equipment.

Radio-equipped Jeep speeds along. Note the canvas side-anti-draught panels – a much desired Jeep necessity.

areas – thus allowing about ten minutes of resistance to water during the 'wading' time it took to leave a landing craft and drive ashore in water of shallow depth – up to five feet deep. Jeeps could even be wrapped in canvas to aid flotation. However a standard, unprotected Jeep could, if driven at the correct speed above 4mph, create a protective 'bow wave', and could be driven through standing water up to a depth of at least three feet without trouble, so long as speed was maintained and not allowed to become excessive.

For the assault-landing amphibious Jeep that could drive or float off a landing craft, a special synthetic coating known as Glyptal was hand-painted on all crucial wires and conduits in the engine bay; such coating or paint insulated vital electrics from water ingress. A snorkel-type air-intake breather was mounted vertically on the windscreen frame – well above water level, to supply air to the carburettor. The engine exhaust was also raised up over the bonnet via metal trunking onto the windscreen frame to avoid the chance of water entering it and clogging the outflow. The Jeep's key mechanical drivetrain components were also coated in a special grease with a high asbestos content. This had to be hand-applied and hand-removed after use in water – risky and time-consuming.

Incredibly, and little known, were the mud-floating Jeeps. These saw large, wide profile rings of steel bolted to the Jeep's main wheel hub and rims to extend its footprint and reduce area-loading, by creating an external, outboard-mounted, grooved metal 'wheel' that allowed the Jeep to traverse mud flats and flooded fields. The official name for this curious system was 'Mud Flotation Adapter'.

Jeeps used in tropical areas, and also in European winters, were also equipped with tyre-chains to increase their traction.

The Ford GPA was a fully bodied amphibious version of the Jeep, designed by Ford in 1942, and called the Seep. Effectively this was a Jeep encased in an external, clad waterproof hull. Produced from 1942 and criticized for its shortcomings, namely a very low freeboard that allowed all-to-easy swamping, it was overweight and unwieldy, and was not deemed a success, but nevertheless did perform in several wartime theatres with 10,000 built and supplied to Allied forces.

The Arctic-type Jeep: For use in extreme conditions likely to disable a crew, Jeeps could be fitted with a hard-top roof that was made of metal and wood. It could be bolted to the tub and had real, secure, side doors. Glazing extended to the rear half of the top. Correctly fitted and weather-sealed, this Jeep addition was much appreciated by troops in Europe and Russia.

The cargo Jeep: This ingenious Jeep was created in the field by soldiers out of wrecked

Jeeps. Welding, nuts, bolts and steel-bashing produced a modified and longer Willys MB-type Jeep. A 4-foot extension to the chassis provided more cargo capacity. A ten-man stretched chassis Jeep was also created by the U.S. Coast Guard, but it had unfortunate handling qualities.

The trailer Jeep: Jeeps were soon fitted with a towing hook and the ¼-ton Bantam trailer K438/A with its light-weight, strong frame; its ability to be overloaded and to float proved ideal as a towed trailer. Jeeps could also tow guns, rocket launchers, howitzers, and gun carriages. The British designed a lightweight trailer type that had a rear towing eye – so trailers could tow trailers – up to four. This created a significant cargo-moving capacity by one Jeep.

The British LRDG/SAS Jeep: A defining armed-assault Jeep concept, these early production Jeeps of 1941 were fitted with a host of handles, hooks, carrying mounts and assorted extras in order to carry fuel tanks, jerry cans, rations, spares, radios, and tyres. Extra radiator cooling came from a condenser unit. The .5-inch Browning and .303-inch Vickers machine guns were both fitted. A Vickers K-Type gas-powered, multi-barrelled machine gun (650 rounds per minute) was also fitted to some of the LRDG Jeeps. By mid-1942 the LRDG had 15 in-service Jeeps; it received newer Jeeps in 1943 that were also fitted with mortars.

The six-wheeled Jeep: Adding six wheels and a longer tub created a Jeep personnel carrier of which very few were built by Canadians at their Army Proving Establishment in Ontario. The same vehicle with tracks created the half-tracked Jeep. Neither entered full-scale production.

The Rotabuggy 'flying' Jeep: This British experiment of 1943 saw an autogyro mechanism fitted to a Jeep and mounted via the central pintle in the cabin floor. Lift was dependent on forward speed turning the undriven rotors. Reliant upon being towed by a powerful aircraft, once airborne, the 'Rotabuggy' provided simple but risky progress. It was flight-tested successfully in November 1943 at Sherburn-in-Elmet. The idea was abandoned in favour of glider-borne deployment of Jeeps for D-Day. The Australian Army also worked on this concept for New Guinea operations and tagged it the 'Fleep'. This used a three-bladed propeller creating more lift than the British two-bladed variant. Some attempt at aerodynamic body fairing also took place. Although thought viable, the need for the short take-off and landing device for use in the jungle was soon overwhelmed by events.

The air-drop Jeep: Airborne deployment of Jeeps needed to be quick and in large

The real- thing – an original unrestored 'Arctic Top' metal/wood-built hard top on the Jeep as seen in several theatres of war including the USSR and Europe.

Of note, this (leading) Jeep has external .30 Calibre armament mounted on the right-hand body side using the chassis outrigger support extension plate.

The railway Jeep. Wider wheels permitted a wider track and the ability to run on standard gauge railway tracks – extremely useful. Wire-cutter bar is also fitted. (Photo: QMC/DoD)

The British Long Range Desert Group as precursor to the Special Air Service used early Jeeps to great effect in the North Africa theatre. Note the radiator condenser unit mounted on the front bumper and the cut-way grill to aid airflow cooling to the engine bay. Extra fuel tankage can be seen on the bonnet and add sides.

RAF-marked Jeeps (in dark blue) were a common sight, not least in occupied Germany and the Berlin sector.

101st Airborne Jeep is arguably a quintessential Jeep marking and this one is exactly correct in its specification, and an MVT regular.

The Ford-built Jeep Seep amphibious variant during its 1940s testing. (Photo: US Army)

Jeep with litter/ stretcher frame added and carrying more than 3 troops. Far East 1944. (photo: US Army Medical Corps)

deployed Jeeps directly into the combat zone – including the Jeep crews – in one go. Men of the 101st Airborne did likewise, notably into the hard winter of the Ardennes battle in late 1944. Jeeps could also be pallet-mounted and parachuted into the combat zone. Many survived such drops with nothing more than bent suspension or a ripple in the body.

In-theatre variations: In the field, local attention and repairs gave rise to non-standard differences in Jeep specifications – especially when a damaged Jeep was repaired using cannibalized components from wrecked Jeeps. Of example, by 1943 during the North Africa campaign, Jeeps in Tunisia were locally fitted with extra carrying brackets for external fuel cans. Additions to the folding roof (tilt), changes to instrumentation, bumper bars, mounts, and seats were all recorded. Of note, Jeeps could be made to run on railway lines via the fitting of the steel wheel adaptors. Australian troops converted Jeeps to railway specification for use in the Far East and British Royal Engineers operated rail wheel-equipped Jeeps between the vital port and Cherbourg and the city of Caen

numbers: enter the use of the American Waco glider and the British Horsa glider. Many major airborne operations in Europe and the Far East saw combat-ready Jeeps deployed from the rear hold of a glider – provided that a successful landing had been made. The Arnhem deployment was the most celebrated British airborne Jeep deployment. The U.S. 82nd Airborne

after D-Day. Jeeps were also fitted with snow plough blades mounted onto the front chassis longerons. Extended mudguards were also locally fabricated to reduce the spray off the front wheels entering the cabin via the tub's cutaway sides.

The British created fabric, weatherproof, glazed side panels to keep the cold out of their Jeep cabins: one enterprising American unit put a salvaged Perspex aircraft cockpit glazing bubble over the top of a Jeep to provide weather protection. British Eight Army officers in North Africa reduced sun and dust exposure by building side panels for their Jeeps out of pallet wood and ration boxes.

The jerry can was a term applied to fuel tanks that the British had acquired from the Germans in place of standard-issue British fuel cans that had proved troublesome and split easily. The 'American' was the standard-issue American Quarter Master Corps fuel tank container – slightly larger than the British or German fuel cans. Both armies it seems preferred the American or the jerry can.

The VIP/General's Jeep: The Jeep was the choice of mount for all the leading Allied military figures during the Second World War. Such special Jeeps featured more comfortable (padded) seats, enhanced radio kit, special pennants and rank badging mounted to the front bumper and bonnet/hood. Weatherproof side panels to the tilt roof were also available for VIP occupants – although the British had fitted weatherproof side doors and panels to their 'all-ranks' Jeeps early on (as fabricated by the Humber Car Company). Mudflaps and extended mudguards also featured on the 'General's' Jeeps. From private soldiers and sergeants through to lieutenants, captains, majors, colonels, brigadiers and generals of various star ratings, the Jeep was the transport of choice.

HRH Queen Elizabeth (Queen Mother) was seen driving a Jeep during the war. At the Casablanca Conference in 1943, President Roosevelt toured U.S. troop lines in Morocco in a Jeep. At Yalta in 1945, he used a specially modified Soviet Lend-Lease Jeep.

General MacArthur used his personal GPA throughout the Pacific campaign – notably in the Philippines. General Stilwell used a Jeep (with an Indian driver) in Burma – as did Merrill's Marauders in Burma 1944. General D. D. Eisenhower rode in General Patton's Jeep – the one with full-height weatherproof side-door panels and extra mudguards.

Lieutenant-General Mark Clark entered Rome in a Jeep as the U.S. Fifth Army went north through Italy. Field Marshal B. L. Montgomery, commander of the British 21st Army Group, often chose to use a Jeep instead of his Humber staff car.

Lieutenant-General G. S. Patton used the Jeep in North Africa, Sicily, and again

Details of canvas 'tilt' roof and rear valance equipment.

as the U.S. Third Army entered Germany in late 1944. His Jeep had a padded, red leather seat, and brass air-horns on the front.

In Normandy, before his death, Brigadier-General. T. Roosevelt, Jnr., the assistant commander of the U.S. 4th Infantry Division, used a Jeep named the 'Rough Rider'. Major-General M. D. Taylor, commander of the 101st Airborne Division, drove his open Jeep in northern France. General O. Bradley, commander of the U.S. 12th Army Group, used a Jeep and presented one to Soviet Marshal I. Konev in Berlin in 1945.

A Canadian general, Major-General Worthington GOC 4th Armoured Division, appears to have had a uniquely modified 'barrel'-topped Jeep with a curved canvas roof and curved side panels with doors fixed to his Jeep's tub. A curved-top infill panel was mounted onto the Jeep's windscreen header rail. Canadian General H. Crerar drove a personal Jeep from 1944.

Admiral C. W. Nimitz, CIC U.S. Pacific Fleet was presented with an ex-Army Jeep for his personal use after the naval victory at Midway. The vehicle was painted in spare U.S.N. Grey.

Winston Churchill toured Berlin in a Jeep in 1945 – interestingly it was equipped with both British, American, and Soviet documents and passes upon the windscreen. General de Gaulle entered liberated Paris in a Jeep, and General Leclerc toured Indochina in 1945 in a Jeep equipped with an armoured windscreen.

Latterly, at the end of the first Indochina war, the victorious Viet Minh, in an act of supreme irony, used a Jeep to drive into Hanoi.

Other variants: Military Police, U.S. Coast Guard, USAAC/USAAF airfield operations and rescue vehicle, H.Q. Transport, Bomb Disposal Squad, RAF Ground Operations, Berlin Zone Transport, Soviet Transport.

This 1945 Ford-built Jeep shows the rare windscreen header rail extension panel that allowed a higher canvas roof fitting. Unrestored and original, this highly prized spec of Jeep is typical of the kind now forming the basis of the restoration movement framed by specialists such as AMD 4x4 in the UK who own it.

Above left: Jeeps, even ones from California, rust, and require much restoration and fettling. This one is typical of the current original, unrestored-Jeep marketplace.

Above right: The restoration and re-enactment movement provides the Jeep enthusiasts and the modeller with much scope. This Jeep fly's the correct flag! Note the winch on front-end and the rope stowage details.

Centre left: Jeep line-up depicts various markings.

Bottom left: Willys Jeep on the road at pace.

England 1944. Medical convoy ready for deployment. Note the Jeep has early Slat-grille and special livery. (Photo: US Army Air Corps)

Below top: Willys command post. Note the electric wiper motor on the header rail and goggles.

Below bottom: British markings on a 1943 Willys-built Jeep.

The wartime Jeep served across the globe, it lived beyond its creators' wildest dreams, like barely a handful of other mechanical military-use devices, Jeep mechanized the Allies, delivered significant personnel, material, and firepower, and affected the course of the war. Jeep was a defining achievement and an example of great design and continuing ingenuity. Jeep has in fact outlived its design, its purpose and yet it continues to have its effect. How many other vehicles can claim such a record?

Post-War Developments

The original GP/Jeep design lived on after 1946 as a French-produced device of Hotchkiss renown.

Hotchkiss of France (Hotchkiss-Brandt of Paris) secured the rights to build Jeeps in France and manufactured 27,604 such vehicles for French military use through to the 1960s.

Often-forgotten was the Japanese Mitsubishi licence for Jeep manufacture in post-war Japan. In South America, Willys-Overland do Brasil, began building Jeeps under licence in Brazil in 1954. The Jeep Station Wagon was marketed from 1958 (it was no longer contemporary in the U.S.) under the name of the 'Rural Production' in the Philippines. Jeep derivatives were also manufactured in Brazil, India, and other parts of Asia. Today, restored Jeeps also see Hotchkiss hybrids, CJ-retro reversions, alongside the true original Jeep series of 1941–46.

For the Jeep, the post-war iterations boasted six-cylinder engines, civilianized models (the CJ-2 series) which created a post-war brand; the first American steel-bodied (non-'Woody') estate car or 'shooting brake' was the Jeep Station Wagon styled by Brook Stevens. The Jeep estate car or wagon was America's first iteration of this idea and quickly sold 6,533 in 1946, and 33,214 in 1947 – despite being based on a light-weight, wartime Jeep chassis. Originally only available with rear-wheel drive, a four-wheel-drive version was marketed in 1949. The fitting of a six-cylinder, side-valve 2,433cc engine, gave the Jeep wagon real performance but a huge thirst.

In 1949 there followed the 'Jeepster' convertible – with a proper mechanically operated weatherproof folding roof and a price tag of nearly $2,000 dollars. Only 22,400 were sold and production ceased in 1951.

Jeeps were fast, nimble, in fact quite sporty as an open two-seater and had the go-anywhere character that could be used on the beach, on a farm or off-road, or just for fun: a ready civil market was assured for the Jeep and its reincarnations across the decades.

Artwork as applied, marked out many a Jeep in theatre. This one is a classic example.

French-marked Hotchkiss-built Jeep reveals few external differences to the wartime Jeep.

Far East 1945, Jeep in service during the occupation forces tenure. Note the unit markings and twin wipers fitted. (Photo: US National Archives)

The Austin Champ was a 1950s interpretation of the Jeep idea designed by Charles Sewell. Austin in America via Bantam in the 1930s certainly missed out, and yet bizarrely created a post-Jeep, post-Land-Rover 4x4 all of its own as the 'Truck/1/4 ton/ 4x4' – but better known as the Champ. At one stage it was to be known somewhat enigmatically as the 'Wolseley Mudlark' .

Authentic Jeep – W. King at the wheel of 101AB marked Willys equipped with rear bustle cage and correct fittings including the radio aerial mounting cover.

Acknowledgements
AMD Four-Wheel-Drive (Restorations)
Military Vehicle Trust (MVT) and MVT North Oxon/Cotswold members
W. King, F. King, T. Gosling
Froude & Hext (Models)

Selected Bibliography / References
AMD Four-wheel-Drive (Restorations) Dawson, M. Personal Communications.
Automotive News, 'How Americans got to meet the Jeep in 1942'
Chrysler / Jeep Press Office.
Department of Defense.
Foster, Patrick R., *Jeep: The History of America's Greatest Vehicle*, Motorbooks, Oscl, WI., 2014.
Fowler, W., *Jeep Goes to War*, Parkgate Books, London, 1998.
Heath, B., *The Automobile*, June 1944 pp. 46-53.
Hogan, Lt. E. P., 'The Story of the Quarter-Ton, The Army's Smallest Car Known as a "Jeep", 1941.
QuarterMaster Corps Operations in the War. Center of Military History: U.S. Army, 1966.
The Quartermaster Association, *The Quartermaster Review. Vol. XXI no. 2*, Washington D.C.
TM 9-803 1⁄4-ton 4x4 Truck (Willys-Overland Model MB and Ford Model GPW), U.S. War Department, 22 February 1944.
U.S. Ordnance Standard Nomenclature List – G-503 (Willys MB/ Ford GPW).
Ware, P., *Military Jeep Manual*: 'An insight into the history, development, production and role of the U.S. Army's light four-wheel-drive', Haynes Publ., UK.